KINGDOM'S EDGE

Look for other books
in the Kingdom Series
by Chuck Black

KINGDOM'S DAWN — BOOK ONE
KINGDOM'S HOPE — BOOK TWO
KINGDOM'S EDGE — BOOK THREE
KINGDOM'S REIGN — BOOK FOUR
KINGDOM'S QUEST — BOOK FIVE
(Spring 2006)

Available Audio Books
KINGDOM'S DAWN
AUDIO BOOK DRAMA — BOOK ONE
KINGDOM'S HOPE
AUDIO BOOK DRAMA — BOOK TWO

www.kingdomseries.com

KINGDOM'S EDGE

Chuck Black

This book is an allegorical depiction of the Christ story that was written for all ages. It is an adventure with deep symbolism that will challenge you to search the Scriptures.

Perfect Praise Publishing

KINGDOM'S EDGE
Second Edition

Manuscript edited by Andrea Black

Illustrations by Marcella Johnson
Copyright © 2002 Perfect Praise Publishing

"Deliverance" music copyright © 2002 by Emily Elizabeth Black
"Deliverance" lyrics copyright © 2002 by Chuck Black

Published by Perfect Praise Publishing
Williston, North Dakota

ISBN 0-9679240-0-6

Printed in the United States of America

Library of Congress Control Number: 2002095476

I dedicate this book to my devoted wife and editor, Andrea, and to my children Brittney, Reese, Ian, Emily, Abigail, and Keenan.

CONTENTS

Preface

This is an epic story about Cedric and his life-changing encounter with the Prince of a distant land. It can be read for the simple joy of an adventure story, but it was written with a purpose of greater significance: to re-spark the interest of readers of all ages in the greatest story ever told. No writer can create a story more profound or more fascinating than the true story of Jesus Christ and his redeeming visit to earth. The full impact of the story in the gospels does not completely grip us until we attain significant spiritual maturity. Thus, as Jesus so often taught in parables to awaken our minds to the deeper truths of his kingdom, I have attempted to help the reader take a fresh look at a story that has transformed lives for twenty centuries and circled the globe thousands of times.

Each chapter was written with specific Scripture in mind and carries greater meaning when God's Word is fresh in our hearts. Therefore, it is recommended that one of the Gospels be read before starting this story.

Hopefully, the reader will identify himself or herself with Cedric and discover adventure in their own walk with the Lord. It is my most earnest desire to bring honor and glory to God through the story penned on the following pages. May your zeal for God's Word be renewed, and may you also be worthy of those welcoming words spoken by Jesus!

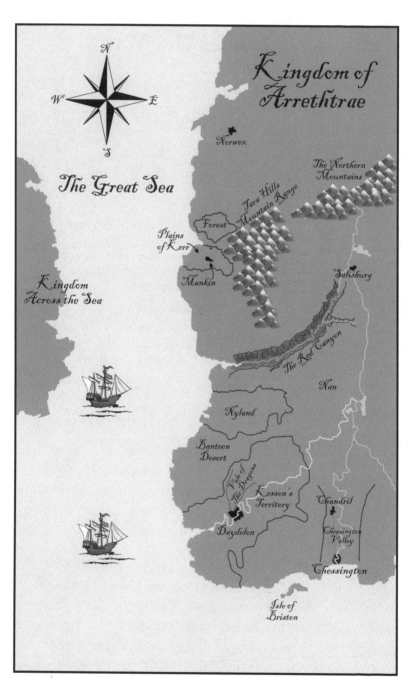

Chapter 1 - "Something Evil Comes Our Way"

My heart is beating rapidly. My eyes are focused. I can see the dust rising in the distance. Something massive and evil is coming our way.

As I scan the horizon from left to right, my eyes come to rest on the line of gallant knights beside me that stretch as far as the eye can see. They are men of courage and valor. Yes, I am in that noble line as well. My steed's muscles twitch with power in anticipation of the coming battle. My armor shines and the helmet fits my brow comfortably. My sword gleams in the sunlight—polished and sharp. I have worked my sword for months in preparation for this very moment in time.

I am an unlikely knight—Cedric is my name. I come from the city of Chessington, in the kingdom of Arrethtrae. A few short years ago you would not believe it is I who tells you this tale of battles, knights, and swords. Time has gone quickly. I remember when I was but a peasant...

"Cedric," called William. "If you don't hurry, we'll miss the procession."

William was a dreamer. Unfortunately, these were times where not even dreamers could hope for a brighter tomorrow. Although his heart was tender, his features were sharp, giving the false impression that he was a hard man. William was strong and knew where he wanted to be, but was not sure how to get there. His hair

11

was dark and matched his brown eyes. Taller than average, he was a handsome man. I had known him since I was a boy. He was my friend.

"William, you know I've got to check on Leinad first. Besides, what is so grand about seeing not-so-noble 'Noble Knights' pass by when my stomach howls in hunger?" I said.

"If we could only *be* one of them, we wouldn't *be* hungry," said William as we approached an old cottage that matched the age of its single occupant.

"You're dreaming again, William," I said. "We were not born of noble blood and we will therefore never become a Noble Knight. Get that foolish notion out of your head!"

Leinad lived just outside Chessington near a small stream that lazily wound its way toward the sea to the south. He was a strange fellow. I had come to know him when I was a young lad. People tend to avoid what they cannot understand or what makes them uncomfortable, and this was the case with Leinad. Although most people avoided him, I was drawn to him and his stories—stories that seemed too strange to be true and too original to be fabricated. If even a small portion of the tales were true, then Chessington was ignorant of a very gallant man. If the tales were indeed made up, then Leinad was just as everyone thought him to be…insane. Either way, I had a tender spot in my heart for him, especially since he was now too old to properly care for himself.

"Good day, Sir Leinad," I raised my voice in greeting as we approached his door. Many of his stories portrayed himself as a knight in service to the King. I half-jokingly addressed him as such, but I could never tell if it was I who was humoring him or if he was humoring me by graciously accepting my flippant use of the title.

"Ah, dear Cedric," came the familiar warm voice. "Welcome to my palace...please come in."

We stepped into his home to see Leinad seated at a small table near the south wall. His left hand was resting on the sill of the window he'd been staring through.

His silver hair and brows partnered with his bent frame to paint a picture of a man near the end of life's journey. He initiated an attempt to rise and meet us, but I halted him as I placed my hand on his shoulder.

"It's alright, Leinad," I said. "I know you are already standing in your heart."

"It is good to see you, Cedric and William," Leinad said with sincerity. He smiled at us with his eyes.

"Hello, Leinad," said William. "How are you feeling today?"

Leinad took in a deep breath, and he turned again toward the window.

"They listened once before, but time has defeated the sincerity of truth." Leinad said, answering a question no one asked.

William glanced my way with a raised eyebrow. I smiled.

"We brought some bread for you, Leinad," I said trying to break his distant trance. "I will try to bring some fruit on my next visit, but the city is pretty short on food these days."

Leinad turned to us and gazed into my eyes. "*Time* is short," he said. "The power of the King is near and the Dark One is mounted. You must be ready...the people must be ready!"

13

We were used to Leinad's odd talk, but today he seemed overcome with his delusions.

"My mission is nearly complete," said Leinad. "The Sword of the King sings in anticipation of the one who is worthy!"

"Yes," I said, "your sword has no equal in splendor or beauty, that is certain. You have done well in its keeping. Leinad, we must leave you now, but I will return in a few days to check on you. We can talk more then."

Leinad smiled condescendingly. "Very well, Cedric. Thank you for the bread. The King will remember your kindness to me."

I bowed and smiled as I winked at William. "Good day then, Sir Leinad," I said as we turned toward the door.

Outside, William took a deep breath and shook his head in pity. "Someday, William, you and I will be hallucinating fools too," I said as we quickened our pace to make the procession.

"I don't think you should humor the old man so much, Cedric," said William as we entered the city.

"What harm can it do, William," I responded. "Leinad is old, and if he wants to spend his final years believing in something more than we are living...then why not?"

"Yes, but I think you crossed the line with that bit about the sword," said William.

"The sword is real," I said nonchalantly and soon was walking by myself. I turned around to see William standing still with a perplexed look.

"What?" came his bewildered reply.

"Yes," I said. "Leinad owns a sword that is more magnificent than any I've ever seen—even more beautiful than any of the swords owned by the Noble Knights."

"Where did he get such a sword?" he asked still not quite believing me.

"His story is long and bizarre, William. In truth I do not know how he came into its ownership," I said. "He keeps it wrapped in a cloth in that old wooden chest in the corner. I fear that someone would kill him for it if they knew it was there. That is why I have told no one about it."

William rejoined me, but his gait was slower now, and his thoughts were deep.

"You're sure about this sword, Cedric?" he asked.

"It's been years, but I've seen it myself," I replied. "It nearly glows in its splendor. Why someone would give a sword like that to Leinad is a mystery indeed."

At the city's main thoroughfare, we pushed our way to the front of the crowd. Beside us, a woman with two small children waited, hoping for a scrap of food the Noble Knights might throw her way. The children's faces were as dirty as their clothes. Poverty overwhelmed the people. The sound of hoofs on cobblestone announced their approach.

"Their horses prance and snort to match the arrogance of their riders," I said in low tones to William.

"Enough, Cedric. After all, these Noble Knights are the chosen, are they not?"

"The King has been gone so long that I wonder if he even remembers this dreadful land," I replied.

A poor old peasant woman was begging from one of the knights as he passed. "Please, good sir, a bit o' food for an old hungry woman?"

He laughed as he threw a half eaten apple her way. "Don't eat it all at once," he sneered. The old woman picked up the dust-laden apple and ate it as though it was her last meal; maybe it would be.

The Noble Knights often passed through the streets handing out tidbits of food to show their "good will" toward the people. I believe they did it to inflate their egos; they loved their position over the people. They were indeed, however, chosen by the King to defend our land. And from all I have heard of the King, he was just and fair. Somehow, since he'd left for another country, the welfare of the kingdom continually declined.

"Here old man, have a feast today." One of the knights threw a loaf of bread to a bent, old man just in front of me. I prepared for my opportunity, fully expecting the feeble old man to miss. I saw his hand reach up for the hurled loaf. The slow, gnarled hand and fingers I expected to see were not gnarled at all. In fact, the hand was quick and strong. He snatched the loaf with such ease and purpose; I looked a fool as my hands grabbed a handful of air.

The old man wore rags that served as a cloak to cover his head and body. He began to turn around. As he did, his back slowly straightened until I faced a man who was a full three inches taller than I. He was not bent, or gnarled, or old. On the contrary, this man was close to my age and had shoulders as broad as a horse. His arms were defined and powerful. One could even see strength in his jaw as he removed the cloth that covered his head.

A man's eyes give away the story of his character, my father once told me. I forced myself to gaze into the

16

eyes of the stranger. I felt as though he had already questioned my eyes for my character. His eyes burned like fire. They penetrated into the very depths of my soul. They were not eyes of hate, or malice—far from it. I saw power, yet meekness, forcefulness, yet gentleness, discipline, yet compassion. I had never seen eyes like his!

He stretched forth his hand with the loaf of bread and offered it to me. I slowly took it from him.

"Tell me, Cedric," spoke the stranger in a rich voice, "what do you hope for?"

My mind was fuzzy. He must have heard my conversation with William, for he spoke my name. I heard the hungered cry of one of the children beside me. How selfish I felt. I was ready to rob an old man of his bread, and instead was given the very thing I'd hoped to take. I knelt down to the child and gave her the loaf of bread. "I'm sorry I haven't more to give you," I told the child's mother.

I turned to the stranger once more. "I am a man of little hope, sir. The kingdom becomes more dreary every day. The people are starving, and the Noble Knights are the only ones who fare well. What is there to hope for? Were I foolish enough to hope, it would be that Arrethtrae were a kingdom free from hunger...a kingdom of truth, justice and honor...a kingdom where men may serve the King as knights, though only common blood flows through their veins...where each man's character determines his worth, not his family name. No—hope and dreams you will not find in my heart, for I am too acquainted with disappointment already. If you're looking for dreams, William here is the one to talk to."

17

"And what are your dreams, William?" asked the stranger as he turned toward him.

William was taken aback by the stranger's gaze, as I was. "You are clothed as a peasant though you hardly look the role. Tell me who you are, sir, and I shall tell you my dreams," said William.

"I am a man from a distant land," said the stranger. "What are your dreams, William?"

William paused. "Well, 'Man From a Distant Land,' I dream of becoming a knight and serving my King as the Noble Knights do."

"And would you also pass out scraps of food to the poor as the Noble Knights do?" asked the stranger.

"I AM the poor, sir," replied William. "I would never forget these people or their demise. I would defend my King and serve his people."

"Well spoken, gentlemen. Do not despair. The King knows the plight of his people in Arrethtrae. I bid you farewell, 'Cedric of Little Hope' and 'William of Dreams.'" With that, the stranger turned and disappeared into the throng of people.

"Well, William," I said, "it looks as though you are not alone in your dream world."

"That man is more than a dreamer, Cedric, and you know it. His peasant clothes don't fool me. There was something about that man!"

"Yes, yes, William. I'm sure he runs a dreamers guild you could join." I laughed and slapped him on the back.

There WAS something about that man, I thought privately.

∽❦∽

Chapter 2 - "The Unlikely Knight"

The days went by and my mind kept returning to the encounter with the stranger from a distant land. *Who was he?*

"I hear the Noble Knights are training in the square this afternoon," said William as we lifted our day's catch onto the dock. "Let's go watch for a bit."

"It's all for show, William," I said. "We've seen them sword fight a hundred times."

"I know, Cedric, but seeing how grand they handle a sword gives me comfort when I think of the Dark Knight and his desire to conquer this kingdom some day."

"Yes, I suppose you're right," I said. "Let's finish up and make an early day of it."

On our way to the square, we detoured to Leinad's home to check on him.

"What do you think of Leinad, William?" I asked as we neared the small old cottage.

"I don't think I can answer that, Cedric," said William. "Calling him crazy doesn't fit, and yet his delusions of past adventures are absurd."

"I know what you mean, William," I said.

We knocked on Leinad's door. "Sir Leinad, may we enter?" I asked through the closed door.

There was no answer. I called to him again...silence. I opened the door hoping to find him asleep but dreading worse. He was not asleep nor was he anywhere in the home.

"William, let's check down by the stream," I said with some urgency. "Maybe he fell while getting water."

Leinad was nowhere to be found. At the stream's edge, an ominous thought invaded my mind. I grabbed William's arm—we had simultaneously come to the same conclusion.

"THE SWORD!" we said in unison and ran back to Leinad's home. We burst through the door and looked for the chest. It was in the corner and still closed, but I saw finger marks in the dust on its lid. I hesitated before opening it for I knew it would tell me the fate of Leinad. I knelt down before the chest…hoping not to find what I knew I would. The hinges creaked as I lifted the lid and gazed inside. The cloth was open, and the sword was gone!

My heart sank, and William placed his hand on my shoulder. "I'm sorry, Cedric," he said sympathetically. "There is a chance he is still alive."

I fought back tears and tried to convince myself that William was right and that Leinad might still be alive. After all, there was no sign of a struggle, no body, and no blood.

"Maybe the sword was stolen while he was away," I said hopefully. "He could have gone into the city for provisions. Although he is old, he is quite determined. Let's get to the City Square and start looking there."

We entered the city, and I was anxious and disturbed. The mystery of Leinad's disappearance weighed heavily on my mind as we arrived at our destination. A large oak tree identified the center of the square. The people were already gathering to see the Noble Knights in action. Before long, thousands of people had assembled. One hundred of the strongest, bravest men in the kingdom comprised the Noble Knights. I had to admit that they looked to be an awesome force with which to reckon. Their armor glistened and the horses stamped their pride of belonging to such a gallant force. The swords were a sight to behold. Each of these knights carried a sword that was the envy of all men. Their sword was the mark of their knighthood, a testament to their skill as a swordsman.

William and I searched the crowd and nearby shops in search of Leinad, but he was nowhere to be found. My hope faded slightly, but I was determined to search the entire city to find him if necessary.

The training of the Noble Knights began and I watched, but my mind found no rest from the mystery of Leinad's disappearance.

Each knight fought another to determine who was the best swordsman. Within minutes of each duel, the best swordsman was obvious. The defeated knight knelt in submission before his victor. Fifty were eliminated in the first round—then twenty-five. Swords screamed through the air and clashed with great force until there was one. The Noble Knight Kifus always won. He was truly the best in the entire kingdom, and he proved it time after time. The people cheered as the Noble Knights encircled Kifus and knelt in honor.

"Thief!" yelled a man behind me near a line of shops that bordered the square.

I turned and saw an enraged shop owner gripping the arm of a girl.

"Thief—she's stealing my bread!" he yelled again.

He grabbed her basket and opened it for all to see. A single loaf of bread was inside. She was guilty, and a hundred witnesses knew it.

The disturbance brought the attention of Kifus and the Noble Knights. They were clearly upset with the interruption of their ritual, but the shop owner sought justice and dragged the girl into the opening. She tried to cover her face and resist, but it was pointless. I had seen her on the streets before—she was pretty. She was a little younger than I. Her auburn hair was mildly curly and hung below her shoulders. Though the faint, torn, remnants of a dress revealed her extreme poverty, it was clear that she tried to keep herself as respectable looking as possible.

"Please…No!" she pleaded with the man as her slender form twisted in an attempt to escape the humiliation of being caught.

How could she have lowered herself to stealing—even in her poverty? I wondered.

Kifus and the other Noble Knights moved toward the man and his captive.

"What is going on here?" asked Kifus with authority.

Kifus and the Noble Knights were the executors of the law. They judged and sentenced all serious disputes and crimes.

"I caught this thief stealing bread from my shop!" exclaimed the man. "Here is the proof," he said as he held forth her basket with the incriminating evidence.

"Is this true?" Kifus asked the young woman sternly.

"Yes, my Lord. But I only—"

"Maggie! Maggie!" A panicked woman burst through the crowd and ran to the girl.

"Please, sir," exclaimed the woman. "Maggie is my oldest daughter, and she stole the bread only to feed her younger brothers and sisters. Please let her go, Lord Kifus," pleaded the mother.

"The law is very clear," stated Kifus. "Anyone caught stealing will lose their right hand! There are no exceptions...not even for your daughter."

The mother appealed again with tears streaming down her face. "I have no way of providing for the children. I have already lost one child to poor health and sickness. Maggie is a good girl. I will serve to repay this man...*please show mercy!*"

Kifus hesitated. He looked at the woman and her daughter and then at the crowd.

"The law must be fulfilled. It is our Code that must be followed," he declared. "Stretch forth her arm on this tree stump!" He commanded his knights.

One knight peeled the girl from her mother's arms and brought her to the stump. Another knight restrained the mother as she clutched her bosom in anguish.

"*No!*" she screamed.

The knight held the girl while another wrapped a leather strap around her wrist and stretched her arm across the stump.

The crowd held its breath as the inescapable arm of the law readied to strike. Kifus drew back his sword and then started its powerful arc across the blue sky toward the delicate hand stretched out on the stump. Her fate was trapped in the steel jaws of the law. There was no pleasant alternative to this ugly episode...I thought!

I saw a man to my right throw back a ragged cloak and I heard the *SHING* of his sword as it left its scabbard. His motion was quick and smooth. The man drew forth a sword that had no equal, not even among the Noble Knights. Its beauty was unmatched and yet familiar. It gleamed so brightly in the sun that it was hard to look upon. Kifus' sword of judgment screamed through air and collided with this stranger's immovable sword of mercy—just above the maiden's wrist. The crowd exhaled in a unified gasp of astonishment.

Who dared to rescue this poor girl from the judgment of the Noble Knights? Who is this man that is either courageous or a fool? The moment seemed frozen in time. The stranger's magnificent sword, powered by mighty arms, held its position under the full strength of Kifus' cut. The young lass opened her eyes in disbelief. She slowly turned her head upward to see the valiant face of her deliverer. Her countenance momentarily revealed absolute shock, then gratitude, and finally fear. She knew that the reprieve from judgment was only temporary, and this brave soul would pay with his life.

"What is that fool doing?" whispered William in my ear.

No one had ever challenged the authority of any Noble Knight, let alone Kifus himself. With his sword still in its protective position above the girl's wrist, the stranger slowly turned his head and locked eyes with Kifus. The rage in Kifus' eyes was evident to all.

"William," I whispered, "doesn't that peasant look familiar?"

"Yes, yes..." recognition came slowly but now William was sure. "It's the stranger we met on the street a few days ago! Why is he doing this?"

"I don't know," I replied, "but look at that sword. It must be Leinad's!"

"Are you sure?" questioned William in hushed tones.

I focused on the sword and tried to remember. It was a long time ago since I'd laid eyes on Leinad's sword. If this man was a thief, he was a strange one. He was risking his life to save the life of a girl…with a stolen sword. I couldn't make sense of it.

"I can't be certain, but I think so," I whispered back. "In either case, I hope he's ready to die. It'll take more than a fancy sword to survive the wrath and skill of Kifus."

Kifus pulled back his sword and glared at the stranger, still absorbing the reality of this rebellious act by a peasant.

Kifus growled at the stranger, "That was a very stupid move, peasant! I don't know from whose castle you stole that sword, but I aim to run you through and return it to its rightful place among nobility. Prepare to die!"

The peasant raised his sword and took a swordsman's stance that caused even Kifus to hesitate. This man was no peasant. He emanated power!

Kifus charged with the full intention of finishing this insolent fool within seconds. The stranger moved to the side with blinding speed, and his sword flashed like lightening to meet Kifus' charge. The impact nearly put Kifus on his face. He regained his balance and approached more cautiously now. Kifus' rage transformed to bewilderment then back to rage. He attacked again. The stranger met every blow and thrust with the perfection of a true master. He nearly teased the Noble Knight Kifus as he maneuvered him at will. We watched in amazement as the flashing swords clashed time after time. Kifus perceived an opening and lunged to finish the stranger, but the stranger parried and executed a bind on Kifus' sword with unmatched speed and power. The fight was over. Kifus stood empty handed, his sword beneath the foot of the stranger.

The crowd, along with the other knights, stood dumbfounded and silent. One question was on the mind of everyone...*who was this man?*

The stranger had disgraced the entire force of the Noble Knights in front of all the people by defeating their very best swordsman. I was still confused, but I knew that a man possessing such incredible skill and courage could hardly be a thief.

In a move of cowardice, two knights drew their swords from behind the stranger.

"Behind you!" I shouted, but my warning was in vain. The stranger had already moved to meet their attack. No one standing in the square that afternoon would have believed a single man could possess such craft as a swordsman were they not there to see it with their own eyes. Within minutes, one knight was without his sword and the other was prone on the ground before the stranger—the tip of the magnificent sword at his throat.

"Release the girl," commanded the stranger. The prone knight looked at Kifus and pleaded with his eyes.

Kifus nodded at the two knights that were restraining the young woman, and they released her. She was too stunned to move—all of her energy was gone. I went to her and helped her gain her feet. She wiped away tears of deliverance as I guided her to her mother who was still held in the shocked grip of a Noble Knight. He finally released her, and Maggie collapsed into the yearning arms of a restored mother.

Kifus spoke. "You are not what you appear to be, sir. Tell us who you are and where you come from."

The stranger relaxed his sword. "I am the Son of the King of this kingdom, and I come from his palace in distant lands across the sea," said the stranger.

A low rumble flowed through the crowd. William came and stood by me. "Could this be true, William? Do you think he is really the King's Son?" I said.

"I don't know, Cedric," said William. "I want to believe it. Like I told you, there is definitely something about that man!"

"If you are the King's Son, give us a sign," Kifus called out. "Show us your royal ring and robe. Where are your servants, the coaches, and treasures worthy of a prince?"

"I can give no sign save my skill as a swordsman and my duty to my Father," replied the stranger.

"Nobility is more than wielding a sword, stranger. It is in the blood. This we know by the Code our King gave us," said Kifus. "We live by the Code!"

"You speak of the Code, yet you do not live by the Code nor teach the people so that they may live by the Code. You dishonor the King by your actions," rebuked the stranger. "The Code of the King is not born in your blood but grown in your hearts. You feed the people morsels of food and keep them in subjection to your whims for the sake of power and control. That is not nobility—it is treachery!"

Never before had anyone dared speak such truth out loud. All that he said made perfect sense. The people were clearly moved as he spoke, and the Noble Knights were growing more furious with every word.

"While you serve yourselves, the Dark Knight prepares this very day for battle against our kingdom," continued the stranger. He turned toward the crowd. "People of

Arrethtrae, my Father has not forgotten you. I come to raise up an army of truth, justice and honor...an army willing to fight and die for the good of the kingdom...an army willing to serve the people...an army that must someday fight the Dark Knight and his Shadow Warriors. I come in the name of the King! I come to serve him and you. Follow me and learn the true ways of the Code."

"You are a traitor to the King!" shouted Kifus. "I will not allow you to destroy his kingdom or his Code!"

The King's Son turned toward Kifus. He raised his magnificent sword at him and the Noble Knights. "*You* have defiled the Code and are not worthy to be called the King's Noble Knights. Be sure of this, I will accomplish my Father's will!" His voice was overpowering. Kifus seemed to shrink from the rebuke.

The King's Son spoke to the people, "I have chosen men among you worthy to serve the King. I do not offer a life of ease and comfort but of sweat and blood. It will not be easy, but it will be noble!"

He moved toward the crowd and closer to us. Soon he was standing before William and me. I looked once more into those penetrating eyes. Was this really happening, or was I in some strange dream? Could this really be the King's Son? I knew in my heart that what he said was true; I saw it in his eyes. This was a man who would not lie. My gaze left his eyes and came to rest on the magnificent sword. It fit his hand as though it were part of him. He followed my eyes.

"Cedric," I heard him speak my name. "Leinad has done well in keeping my sword for this appointed day. Do not worry; your friend is safe."

I believed him and found relief in his words, but why he would entrust such a treasure as this sword to a crazy old man was still a mystery. The golden handle was inlaid with precious stones. Its double-edged blade shined like polished silver and was as sharp as a razor's edge. What a splendid sword it was.

I looked to his face again as he continued to speak. "Will you discover hope and follow me to become a Knight of the Prince, Cedric?"

Me? Surely he was mistaken. "My Lord," I said, "I am but a poor peasant. I am not worthy. Surely you look for someone better than I?"

"No, Cedric, I have chosen you. I do not care about what you were or what you are, but about what you can become."

In my heart I knew I must answer one question—*Do I really believe this man is the Son of the King?* In an instant I knew the answer, and there was but one thing for me to do...I knelt before the Prince. "I will follow you, my Lord."

"And you, William. Will you follow me and discover your dreams?" he asked of my friend.

"My life is yours, my Prince," responded William as he knelt beside me.

"Rise up, my friends, and come with me." His firm hand was upon our shoulders. We rose and followed him through the crowd. The Prince stopped before certain men and bid them to follow him. Most joined us, but some did not. The men he chose were anything but warriors. But who was I to talk? I knew nothing of the skill of sword fighting or knighthood. I had held a sword only once in my life, and it was the very sword that the Prince now wore. Leinad had let me hold it once when I was boy. His tale of the Sword of the King had captivated me, and holding it made the story seem real. I had believed him then but lost that childhood faith later in my "mature" years. Now it all seemed to be happening just as Leinad said. Maybe he wasn't as crazy as I thought.

As we emerged from the crowd, twenty-five men, scruffy men, followed the Prince. The Noble Knights roared in laughter.

"So this is your grand army to defeat the Dark Knight, aye, stranger?" sneered Kifus. "I'm sure your King would be proud of such an awesome selection of knights to defend his kingdom," he mused.

The Prince showed no embarrassment for us as one might expect, but instead turned toward the knights one last time and spoke with authority. "On the appointed day, you will be judged for your treason, and I shall be that judge. My Father has given me all authority over this kingdom—be warned!"

That was the beginning of my life as an unlikely knight. It was a day that changed my life forever.

Chapter 3 - "A Deadly Plot"

L ife was hard. Life was good. Most folks think this a contradiction, but I have learned that the hardest, most difficult times of my life caused the most growth in my character. At the very least, those hard times prepared me for a better future.

The Prince...were the Noble Knights to spend one honest day with him, they would realize how truly noble he is, and that he is indeed the King's Son. He is better with the sword than any man that's laid his hand upon a hilt, past and present, and yet he is not arrogant. His authority as a military commander is unquestioned, and yet he is not harsh. He does not hesitate to destroy evil at its root, and yet he is more compassionate than any man I've seen. He is the King's Son, and yet I have seen him carry a poor, old woman to her home when she was too weak to walk by herself. This is what the Noble Knights hate most about him—he is kind. He is the epitome of what they are not.

We learned the art of the sword from the Master himself, a little each day. He was patient. We studied, and worked, and sweat. We all wanted to become like the Prince. There is a quality about him that draws the good in heart. As we became more proficient, the Prince recruited more men to his army. They too were inept swordsmen at first, but the Master made warriors of them all. We were the Knights of the Prince.

The Noble Knights quickly realized that this stranger was not going away. When they saw his influence over the people, their ridicule became concern. Soon, their concern became a plot.

"William, how was your training today?" I asked as we walked up the narrow streets of Chessington toward the bread stand.

"Well, Cedric, I've been working on some techniques the Prince showed me, but no matter how many times I practice, my skills pale in comparison to his," said William.

"I understand, William. My best work seems a weak imitation of the Prince's," I replied.

We now wore the emblem of the Prince on our tunics. Our swords and scabbards he gave us also bore his mark. We turned the corner and walked up a dimly lit street.

The clink of our swords kept rhythm with our walk. "Good sirs!" came a whisper from the dark.

Dark shadows usually hide dark deeds. We instinctively reached for our swords.

"Who goes there?" I commanded.

"I am but a servant boy—please do not harm me," replied the small voice.

We could not see the boy, but fear was in his voice— that was clear.

"What do you want, lad?" said William.

"I serve in Lord Kifus' house, but I have seen how your leader cares for the people. I come to warn your leader. I overheard some of the knights talking of a plot to kill him. Please warn him. I must go."

We strained to see but only heard the quickened pace of bare feet on cobblestone diminishing to our left side.

"Cedric," said William, "do you think there is any merit to this warning. Are the Noble Knights really that worried about the Prince that they would plot to kill him?"

"That boy was scared. I believe the threat to be real, but plot or no plot, we must tell the Prince immediately."

We found the Prince resting beneath a sprawling tree on a knoll east of the city. This was a place of solitude he'd come to love.

"Good Prince!" I exclaimed. "I am sorry to disturb you, but we have news you must hear at once."

"Yes, Cedric," replied the Prince, "please tell me your urgent news."

I caught my breath from the climb up the hill. "A young servant boy who serves in Kifus' house overheard talk of a plot to kill you! We were not able to validate the source but thought it wise to at least warn you."

The Prince did not seem uninterested, but he certainly was not alarmed by our message.

"Do not worry, my friends. I am not through preparing you or my army. The King's work must be completed. I will not allow Kifus or any of the Noble Knights to interfere," said the Prince.

"But my Lord," said William, "shouldn't we prepare somehow in the event there is truth in this warning?"

"Cedric. William. There is coming a day when I must return to my Father's distant kingdom."

"My Lord, may we come with to serve you there?" I asked hopefully.

"No, Cedric," came his firm reply. "You and the Knights of the Prince must continue what I have started here. Upon you I place my trust. There is one coming who is far more destructive than Kifus or his knights. Leinad warned the people, but their apathy has left them weak."

William and I locked eyes in astonishment. *Leinad?* I thought. *My old crazy companion wasn't really crazy? That means that all of those bizarre stories were...*

"Yes, Leinad was highly favored by the King," replied the Prince in response to our obvious amazement. "He was a mighty and faithful knight, but the kingdom slowly began to ignore him and my Father's warning until Leinad was all but forgotten. Now the Dark Knight is strong and anxious to conquer Arrethtrae...the kingdom is in peril. That is why you must continue to recruit and train men to fight the Dark Knight. He is evil and powerful. When you have established our army of truth, justice, and honor, the Dark Knight will come to destroy you."

He paused for us to digest what he'd just spoken. It was hard to hear this plan. What strategy was this? Why would he leave us when we needed him most?

The Prince continued, "But do not fear. I will come back for you and bring you into my Father's kingdom to complete your training. Then, we will return to this kingdom to utterly destroy the Dark Knight and his Shadow Warriors once and for all. I will lead you to certain victory! I will be king here, and you will help me rule."

He seemed so sure of himself and of the future. It was clear he knew his enemies well, but I have yet to see even the best-laid plan executed without a few major flaws. Yet, there was something about this man!

"You must remain true to the Code. It will carry and preserve you when you think you cannot go on. Do not just memorize the Code...*live* the Code. Will you trust me, gentlemen?"

I glanced toward William. His face was solemn, but his eyes were set on the Prince. We had seen the strength of the Prince when all odds were against him. Why should we doubt him now?

"We trust you though it cost our very lives, my Lord," said William. We knelt before the Prince to confirm our vow.

"Rise and eat with me, good knights," said the prince, and he offered bread and fruit.

While we ate, the Prince spoke. "Listen closely...besides the Knights of the Prince, I have established a secret force in the land comprised of true and valiant knights from my Father's distant kingdom. These men are skilled in the art of the sword and in the art of stealth and disguise. My Silent Warriors will help you in your most desperate times when I am not with you. When you call, 'The King reigns—and his Son', should any be near, they will come to your aid."

"Are there many of the Silent Warriors in the kingdom, my Prince?" I asked.

"More than your eyes will see, Cedric," came his reply. "They are mighty men. I once led them in battle against the Dark Knight and his Shadow Warriors many years ago in my Father's kingdom. The battle was fierce. We defeated them but did not conquer. The Dark Knight and most of his Shadow Warriors escaped. That is why they are preparing to attack this kingdom...they want *revenge!*"

Chapter 4 - "A Desperate Fight"

Our training continued each day. Once we mastered a particular technique, the Prince challenged us with a new, more difficult one.

I parried an oncoming thrust to the left. "Rob, your skill with the sword is impressive. You've improved dramatically since we last fenced," I said to a fellow knight as we trained.

Rob caught my vertical cut and countered with a quick side slice. "Aye, and yours as well, Cedric. Remember though, it was only the third day of training when we first took up our clumsy swords and flung them at each other."

Rob was also one of the first men chosen by the Prince on that spectacular day seven months ago in the square. Rob was offensive to me at first. He was quite rude and brash, but I quickly saw a genuinely kind heart within him. The more I got to know him, the more I liked him. His red, curly hair and fair complexion seemed always accompanied by a boyish grin.

"Yes, I remember well. The Prince is more than a teacher, for it took a miracle to make swordsmen out of us," I said as I caught his slice and countered with my own.

"He is indeed a miracle worker, Cedric, in more ways than one," replied Rob.

"What do you mean?" I questioned.

Rob parried my thrust this time, and the flats of our swords met midway.

"Well," said Rob, "haven't you seen the joy on the faces of the people? He has promised to heal this country and restore their dignity, and they believe him! I know this much, if any man alive can do it, he'll be the one."

Having finished the session, our swords found rest in our scabbards.

"I believe you're right, Rob," I said. "The Prince seems to have all the ingredients to make just such a thing happen."

That evening, William and I passed by a small shop on our way home. We heard quite a ruckus from within the shop and decided to investigate. As we opened the door, there was a part of me that wished we had chosen to walk on and ignore this place. There were two other occupants inside the room besides ourselves. One, whom I presumed to be the owner of the shop, was white and pale. I do not know if his appearance was from the evident fear on his face or if it was a result of the lack of blood due to the large hand that nearly encircled his neck. The other occupant owned the threatening hand and a large hulking body to go with it. His back was to us, but it was enough to know he commanded enormous strength. The large beast of a man heard us enter and turned his head slightly.

"If you want to live, leave this place!" His voice was deep and gruff. The mere sound of it was as threatening as his form.

It was then that I saw that the shop owner's feet were not even touching the ground. Pain joined his face with the fear that we first saw.

"Release this man or face our swords," I replied as boldly as my own fear allowed.

I saw the grip tighten slightly on the shop owner before he threw him into a corner as though he were a rag doll.

"Don't move!" spoke the huge man to the shop owner. He slowly turned to face us, revealing all of his horrific grandeur. He stood nearly seven feet tall. His stringy hair hung to his shoulders partly hiding a deep scar that swept from his left cheekbone down to his chin. His eyes were dark and filled with poisonous hate. His neck joined his shoulders and chest in a mass of muscle. His arms were as thick as a young cedar tree. The hand that encircled a neck just seconds ago now encircled a deadly gleaming sword. He was an ominous sight to behold, indeed. But even this did not chill me as much as what I saw next. His tunic bore the mark of the Dark Knight...he was a Shadow Warrior!

So this was a glimpse of the evil force spoken of by the Prince. I prayed it would not be my last glimpse of life itself.

His voice was thick with indignation, "You will regret this night—now you die!"

He attacked us so violently and forcefully that I feared he would spill our blood with hardly a fight. His blows were incredibly powerful. We retreated slightly to regain ourselves and spread apart to divert his attack. William caught a slice across his arm that bled but was not deep. I pressed an attack to bring the brute off William.

How could we escape with our lives let alone bring justice to this criminal? I truly believe the shop owner would already be dead by now had we not invaded the scene.

It was William that brought some hope to our cause as I saw him advance with a combination that was taught to us by the Prince. In the throes of the Shadow Warrior's fierce attack, I was so preoccupied with defending myself that I had neglected to rely on the training that the Prince so diligently taught us for just such an encounter. I was prepared physically but not mentally.

We tightened our positions and ever so slowly began a methodical advance that soon had the Shadow Warrior on the defensive. His eyes spewed hate, but I saw surprise momentarily cross his face. He renewed his fighting and we gave, but only temporarily. Advance—retreat. Advance—retreat. Were it not for two of us versus one of him, the fight would have ended abruptly. Instead, the fight wore on.

The shop owner was still a puddle in the corner. I did not know if he was dead, or if he feared that the Shadow Warrior was toying with us and thus dared not move.

For all we were worth, William and I could not bring this brute down. We were tiring, and the Shadow Warrior seemed as though his energy was inexhaustible. I knew we were slipping. The Shadow Warrior knew it too.

"You fight like my enemy of old," his voice growled at us. "Tell me who your trainer is before I end your miserable lives."

A floorboard creaked at the entrance of the shop. Our backs were toward the door. My heart sank. Had another Shadow Warrior entered from behind us? Was this to be our end?

"I am!" came the familiar voice of the Prince in response to the Shadow Warrior's question.

At last, I thought. With three of us, we will have a chance of defeating the massive warrior. What a foolish thought it was.

For the first time, I saw fear on the face of the Shadow Warrior. Not just a glimmer of fear, but fear that comes from deep within and stays. His fight immediately left him. The once flashing, powerful sword now hung limply in his hands.

"I know who you are 'Son of the King.'" Even the voice of the Shadow Warrior revealed his fear.

William and I slowly backed off in amazement. This Shadow Warrior could defeat any one of the Noble Knights within seconds, including Kifus, yet the mere sight of the Prince turned him into a cowering fool. It was at this moment that I began to realize how truly awesome the Son of the King must be.

The Prince placed his hand on his majestic sword. The Shadow Warrior withdrew two steps, his sword still lowered.

"Let me live," came a weak, gruff plea from the Shadow Warrior.

"Lay down your sword and go!" commanded the Prince.

The Shadow Warrior did not hesitate. He dropped his sword and moved quickly toward the door. His eyes never left the Prince until he was safely in the street. He turned and ran into the darkness.

The shop owner threw himself at the feet of the Prince. "Thank you, my Lord. You have saved my life this night!"

"What is your name?" asked the Prince.

"My name is Barrett, my Lord," said the shop owner.

"Rise up, Barrett." The Prince lifted Barrett by his arm. "Tell me, how did you fall victim to the likes of this gruesome man?"

Only now was the color coming back to Barrett's face. He started to talk but coughed and choked on his words. I offered him water as he tried to regain some composure.

Barrett was slightly shorter than I with an average build. His coffee colored hair had receded to the top of his head, and his face was clean-shaven. His eyes darted left and right in nervous repetition. I did not know if this was a life-long mannerism or a consequence of his recent near death experience. Barrett was ready to try once again.

"A few months ago, this same man entered my shop and offered to buy my geese and fish at a price higher than I could get from anyone in the city. His only demand was that I tell no one about him or our exchange. He seemed fair enough, so I took his offer. A few days later, he returned with nearly the same offer, so I agreed, since the price was still higher than the street market price. This continued for some time, but each time his price got lower and his demeanor became more fierce. Before long, he demanded the food at a fraction of the market price and threatened me and my family if I didn't agree."

Barrett paused and took another sip of water. He took a deep breath and continued.

"Eventually, I was giving him the food, and he was also demanding money as well. I told the Noble Knights, but they seemed too afraid to even confront him. I do believe he would have killed me tonight had these gentlemen not intervened. Thank you for your bravery, kind sirs. Please take this money in payment for your services." The shop owner offered a bag that jingled with the sound of coins—coins the Shadow Warrior had hoped to steal.

"We accept your thanks but not your payment, Barrett," I said. "We cannot receive money for doing what is honorable and just."

Barrett turned toward the Prince again. "My Lord, how can I be sure this brute will not return?" The fear surfaced once again in Barrett's face.

"If he returns, Barrett, you can be sure he will not return alone. He will bring other warriors more fierce and wretched than himself with him," said the Prince. Barrett looked desperate.

"There is only one way you can protect yourself and your family," continued the Prince. "Follow me, and I will train you, equip you, and protect you."

"I will follow you this very night, my Lord," said Barrett with renewed hope in his eyes that only moments ago were full of fear and desperation.

It was clear to both William and me; we still had much to learn from the Prince!

Chapter 5 - "Master of the Sword"

W e were not experts with the sword by any stretch of the imagination. However, the Prince felt we had learned enough of the sword to add armor to our training.

On one particularly warm afternoon, the Prince chose to teach a few of us how to effectively use the shield.

"It is your shield that will protect you when your enemies fire their flaming arrows at you," said the Prince. "It will stop the deadly blows of his ax and sword. I gave each of you a shield. Take good care of it, for the enemy may strike when you least expect it."

Two hours passed. At first, the shield seemed awkward and clumsy in my hand. But soon, it was natural to hold and to use. I enjoyed the feeling of security it provided.

I was so engrossed with my training that I did not even see them coming. Three of the Noble Knights descended from a hill toward the south of us. Their swords were drawn and they attacked quickly. Although I was surprised, the Prince was not. He was always ready. He had already positioned himself for the onslaught with his shining sword in hand.

These Noble Knights were three of the best. I recognized them from the training they conducted frequently in the square. My initial reaction was to flee. There were four trainees, and we were no match for the Noble Knights, not yet anyway. Despite my instinct to run, I raised my sword for the fight, as did my companions.

"Stand down, gentlemen," said the Prince. "This is my fight."

It was clear he was right, for the Noble Knights focused exclusively on the Prince. We did not seem to pose a threat to them at all. We watched, but did not sheath our swords. We had pledged our lives to the King's Son, and this could be the day to make good our vows.

"Cedric," called the Prince, "your sword."

I tossed my sword fifteen feet to the Prince. As my sword was mid-flight, the Prince turned to his right to engage the first approaching knight. A split second later, the Prince snatched the flying sword blindly with his left hand and brought it to bear on the second knight. His timing and reaction were perfect.

The knights fought with cautious tenacity; they knew of the Prince's skill as a swordsman. They tried to encircle him, but the Prince prevented it. He moved quickly toward a hill that rose up out of the flat ground we were training on. The rise was steep enough such that a man could not easily climb it nor fight from its slope. With the steep terrain at his back, the Prince forced the Noble Knights to engage him head on.

The swords flashed through the air with deadly cuts. I studied the face of the Master as he fought, but I found no panic or fear at all. His jaw was set and his eyes focused, as though they were weapons themselves.

"You have committed crimes of treason against the King," said one of the knights. "We are here to end your traitorous deeds!"

"If you truly knew the King, you would also know me and why I am here," responded the Prince. "You have become ignorant and foolish in your ways. I am here to reestablish my Father's kingdom of honor, truth, and justice…to restore the true meaning of the Code in Arrethtrae."

The three knights formed a semi-circle around the Prince. It seemed hopeless, but I knew not to underestimate the skill of the Prince; he had surprised me many times before. He parried with his left sword and attacked with his right.

Each knight looked for a breach in the defense of the Prince. Surely with his concentration split on three grand knights, he would make a mistake and it would soon be over. They found none. To this day I have never seen a sword fly so swiftly. He met each thrust with absolute precision. The harder the Noble Knights tried, the quicker his sword flew to meet each stroke.

It was the knight to the Prince's right that made the first mistake. Thinking he saw an opening, he thrust forth with all his might, fully expecting to feel his sword meet flesh and bone. The Prince finished glancing a vertical cut from the center knight and met the knight's thrust from the front, causing the sword to pass behind the Prince's back. The knight was now overextended and slightly off balance. The Prince struck a blow to his head with the gold handle of his sword, which knocked him to the ground unconscious.

The two remaining knights pressed harder, anxious to finish the fight. The knight to the left saw a high

45

vertical cut approaching the Prince from his partner and timed a knee level slice to coincide with its arrival. The Prince pulled his left sword off the knight delivering the knee high slice and met the vertical cut from the front in the crux of a cross formed by his two swords as he jumped to escape the knee cut. The low sword passed beneath him, and the Prince planted a forceful heel into the chest of the knight on his left. The knight stumbled back and fell.

The Prince landed and turned on the remaining knight with both swords. Stark fear clouded the Noble Knight's face as he realized his fate was completely in the hands of this "traitor." The knight put forth his sword to defend himself from the impact of two swords, each one commanded by arms more powerful and skilled than either of his own. In one powerful blow, the Prince cross cut both swords with such force that it sheared the knight's sword in two!

The Noble Knight stood dumbfounded and afraid. The knight that had fallen was now on his feet and slowly moving toward the Prince and the sword-less knight. The Prince placed a sword at the neck of the knight he'd just beaten and moved him toward the approaching knight with the edge of his blade.

"Drop your sword," spoke the Prince.

These knights were not used to being humbled, but better judgment prevented the knight from meeting a senseless death. He dropped his sword.

"Take your unconscious friend and leave," said the Prince, "and tell Kifus he must do his own dirty work in the future."

As they turned to pick up the other knight, one of the knights turned back toward the Prince. "Are you truly the King's Son?" he asked genuinely.

The Prince studied his face and said, "What does your heart tell you?"

The Noble Knight was only silent—he was disturbed. They turned and left.

Chapter 6 - "The Tear"

William, Rob, and I walked with the Prince through the streets of Chessington one morning before our training began. The crisp air and fresh sunrise were drearily overshadowed by the clear absence of joy. The sounds of playful, giggling children were replaced by moans of hunger as they rummaged for a scrap of food. The early morning song of motherhood was exchanged for the wail of a suckling babe with no milk to drink. I longed to leave these wretched streets, for I could not bear the pain. But the Master lingered in solemn silence.

"My Lord," I said softly, "shouldn't we be on our way to begin our training?" I'd hoped to move on to the country, away from these desperate, hopeless avenues of despair.

As the Prince turned toward me, I saw deep sadness in his face. A tear fell from his cheek and was swallowed by the dust at our feet.

"Your training is here today, Cedric," said the Prince. "Bring the rest of my knights here as quickly as you can."

"Yes, my Prince," I said. We left at once and found the rest of our brothers at the training site.

When we returned, I was once again astonished by what I saw. The Prince was sitting on a stump of wood with children all around him listening to a story he was telling. Two were sitting on his lap. Children! Children covered in dirt and filth. Why would the mightiest warrior in the kingdom waste time with children! It seemed like such a contradiction. Power, might, strength, and wisdom matched equally with kindness, compassion, and gentleness, all in one man—the King's Son.

He finished the story with the children before addressing us.

"Gentlemen, you will feed these people," commanded the Prince.

We looked at each other rather stupidly, trying to decide if we'd heard right.

"How many people, my Lord?" asked Rob.

"All of them," spoke the Prince.

Although I had seen many amazing things by the Prince, I don't believe I was alone in thinking that he had crossed the line of rational thinking. There were thousands of poor people, maybe more. How could we possibly provide for such a mass of hunger?

"My Lord," said William, "I told you I will never forget the poor, and I won't. We will gladly feed them if there is some way, but you are asking the impossible."

"Today, William, you will begin to fulfill your duty in remembering the poor. You all will, for this is the meaning of the Code," said the Prince. "Go to the docks. There you will find ships full of provisions sent from my Father at my request. Organize yourselves in teams of two, and deliver these provisions to each home. Do not miss a single household."

It was just as the Prince said. All of the knights worked day and night until every home had food. It was glorious work. None of the knights complained at the labor but instead stepped with light feet as each delivered the food. The people wept with gratefulness.

We wept with joy. Children jumped with glee at such a grand gift.

Compassion that acted—I had never seen its equal.

Chapter 7 - "No Escape"

We have learned much. In nine short months, the Prince raised us from the depths of poverty torn peasants to the heights of knighthood. The Prince spent as much time teaching us how to honor the Code and the King as he did on how to handle our swords.

As we learned more from the Prince, we learned more about him. There was something divine in his nature. I feared him for his power. I revered him for his skill. I followed him for his wisdom, but I served him for his goodness. How was it possible that one man could touch another man's life and change it so drastically? I was no longer Cedric the peasant. I was Cedric, Knight of the Prince. This honor did not come because I was able to make a knight of myself, but because the Prince chose to make a knight of me. *Why me?* The question would not leave my mind.

The sun scorched the countryside, but we pressed on with our training. We broke mid-afternoon to quench our thirst and eat bread for nourishment. Beneath the shade of a small grove of trees, the Prince spoke.

"Gentlemen, I am pleased with your training. You are all capable warriors now. You must fully understand the meaning of the Code and bury it in your hearts. To live by the Code is to love and serve the King, and to love and serve each other. Without the Code, your newly found skills with the sword are meaningless and will eventually destroy you. Remember what I have taught you. You must recruit and teach others. My words will guide you in the future."

Sadness fell upon me as I listened between his words. Why did these words sink my heart so? Surely this was not the end.

"My time with you is over." The Prince spoke the words I dreaded to hear though he had warned us of this day.

Emotions of shock and fear swept over our assembly. Whispers and murmurs rose in volume.

"What do you mean, my Prince?" asked a fellow knight.

"Your training is complete," said the Prince. "I have received word from my Father and must return to his kingdom. One day, I will send for all of you, and you will come and feast with me in his kingdom. But for now, your work is here."

"My Lord," protested another knight, "we have so much more to learn from you. We cannot possibly be prepared to take on the Dark Knight and his—."

The knight's words were interrupted by a thunderous noise that only grew louder with each passing moment. It came from the north. No, it was from the west. No, it surrounded us from all sides. The sound of the pounding of horses' hoofs engulfed us from all directions. We drew swords and looked for a place of retreat but found none. Fear came as quickly as the horses.

One hundred Noble Knights with their mounts soon encircled our position. The countenance of Kifus made clear their intention was one of war. We were outnumbered nearly four to one, and they were mounted. *Today we die*, I thought to myself.

"Be still!" came the confident voice of the Prince.

"Today your lies and blasphemies end," declared Kifus. "Your death and the deaths of your petty servants will restore order to this kingdom once and for all!"

"Remember, my knights," said the Prince to us, "your fight is with the Dark Knight and his Shadow Warriors. This is not your time."

The Prince walked toward Kifus without his sword drawn. If this battle were to happen, I knew we would all die. Our fight would be noble but futile. Only the Prince had the power and skill to defeat these vicious opponents. At least he would survive. I knew this to be true.

Midway in the gulf between Kifus and our men, the Prince stopped and spoke. "Kifus, your grievance is with me, not my men. Spare the needless spilling of blood and let my men leave peacefully. I will come to you unarmed as your captive."

The Prince knew we would not survive the fight. Surrender meant certain death for him. He had the power to live; yet he offered his life for us. Why didn't he heed our warning? How could a man this wise allow such a thing to happen? I did not know what to feel. Gratitude, anger, humiliation, and fear meshed together leaving only an impending feeling of defeat.

Kifus sat smugly on his horse, enjoying the moment of power and control. He knew he'd won. Revenge for his humiliation at the sword of this impostor obviously tasted sweet. He hesitated with arrogance, though I knew deep down he was relieved that he did not have to face the Prince's sword again.

"So let it be," said Kifus. "Make way!" He gave his men the order.

Behind us, the circle of mounted Noble Knights broke open to allow passage. No one moved. How could we abandon the Master we came to love, trust, and serve?

"Gentlemen," said the Prince, "you must leave. Remember the Code. Live the Code. Continue the Code, or all that I have done is for naught. Leave in peace."

One by one, the Knights of the Prince turned and walked through the circle of certain death. My own cowardice caused me to turn and leave. Once beyond the break, we ran like frightened, homeless children. I was ashamed!

From the crest of a hill, I peered and saw a dreadful scene unfold. The deadly circle of Noble Knights hesitated in their advance as the Prince drew his sword. He looked down at its beauty and then to the hills. Kifus reached for his sword, but it was not needed. The Prince drew back and threw the magnificent sword into the sky. It slowly rotated end over end through its journey, and the sun occasionally gleamed off its steel as it arched high above the Noble Knights and beyond the clearing. It disappeared far into the thick trees and brush of the forested hills.

The Prince had chosen a silent surrender. The Noble Knights collapsed on him. The powerful hands of the Prince were empty.

Chapter 8 - "A Time to Weep"

I tried to awaken from this bad dream, but morning did not come. Our small group of would-be-knights had scattered. We feared for our lives now. Once they eliminated the Prince, nothing would stop the Noble Knights from hunting us down and executing us for treason. Our strength and confidence abandoned us when we abandoned the Prince. I was back in my peasant rags, attempting to hide. Now I was poor, hungry, and hunted. Worse than all, I was alone. It was a loneliness that surely would last forever.

I sat beneath the shade of an awning just off the street where I first met "the stranger." So much had transpired since then. Two men were talking as they passed by.

"The hangin' is this afternoon," I heard an old man say to another.

"I knew that stranger was an impostor all along," spoke the second man. "Kifus should 'ave strung 'em up a long time ago."

"Maybe," said the first, "but I didn't see you complainin' when he was handin' food to ya!"

"Hey, anytime there's a free lunch to be had, I ain't gonna complain, but it don't mean I believed what he said." The first old man spit to emphasize his disgust.

"Still, I don't see how such a man..."

The words faded with distance, along with my thoughts.

I began questioning my own belief in the Prince. If he truly were the King's Son, why would his life stop at the end of a rope tied by the very men sworn to serve the King? Nothing made sense anymore. My mind ran through thick fog searching for clarity but found none. I wanted the earth to open up and swallow all evidence of Cedric, the peasant.

The square was packed with people. Near the center was the large oak tree. I forced my eyes to search, and I found it—from one of the large limbs hung a rope. I found a corner between two buildings and faded into the shadows, as did my heart.

Kifus led his death procession of Noble Knights around the perimeter of the square, displaying the Prince as though he were some prize catch of the day. His hands were bound, and his head was bruised and beaten. His back was bleeding. My soul was tormented to see him this way. Some people were laughing and jeering; some were crying. *Why? Why was this happening?* I could not bear it any longer and hid my face in the brick and mortar of the wall. I stole a last glance and caught the eyes of the Prince looking my way as they passed.

Even now, on the eve of his death, I saw no fear in his eyes. What I saw was tender compassion. The true power and strength of this man was in his great ability to love in spite of all tragedy. Now, I fully understood the Code. The Prince lived the Code. The Prince *WAS* the Code.

My doubts were gone, but my despair was not. I felt so helpless. He saved my life once. Now he was dying for me, and there was nothing I could do but watch.

Kifus led the Prince to the oak tree, placed him on a horse, and slipped the rope about his neck.

Where was the army of the King to save his Son from death? Didn't he care? Did he even know the peril of his Son? Where were the Silent Warriors?

Kifus spoke loudly for all to hear. "People of Arrethtrae, this man is guilty of treason against the King and against you. He has lied to you and misled you. He brings chaos to the kingdom. Today, justice is served!"

Kifus slapped the horse, and the Prince hanged. No army, no help, only silence. It was a silence that gripped the people as we watched our hope of a better kingdom die with this man.

I turned and ran to the hills. The trees and sky were blurred from my tears. I ran until I felt my lungs would burst. At last I collapsed beneath a sprawling tree. The tall grass swallowed my body, and I wept bitterly. It truly was all over!

Chapter 9 - "A New Beginning"

The sun was nearing the horizon before I found enough energy to move my body. My tears were gone and so was my hope. I raised myself to my knees and wiped away the trails of dirt on my face. *What now?* I wondered. My head hurt and my soul was empty.

Still on my knees, I looked over the grass and brush and came to the realization that my blind run had brought me to familiar country. Our training area was nearby. I moved to stand up, but my eyes caught a glimpse of the unbelievable. Just an arms length before me was the sword of the Prince, its blade embedded into the soft soil. In my grief, I had fallen just short of the sword. I stood and pulled the sword from the ground and held it before me in open palms. The memories of the Prince came back to me like a flood.

"Why did you have to die?" I asked out loud, knowing that I would never find an answer.

"Cedric, what are we going to do?" William tried to break into my muddled thoughts as I stared at nothing in particular.

William was as confused and afraid as I. Most of the Knights of the Prince were scattered, but we managed to meet with a dozen fellow knights in secret. Barrett's shop had a back room with no windows. We locked the doors and spoke in hushed tones.

"Yes, Cedric, what happens now?" asked Rob. "Do we try to get to another city or flee the kingdom altogether?"

"No," I finally spoke. "First we must honor the memory of the Prince and give him a proper burial."

"What?" exclaimed Rob. "Are you mad, Cedric? The Noble Knights have purposely left his body hanging from that tree as a message to all people. If we try to take him down, we'll be found out and killed immediately!"

"Not if we go now, Rob," I said. "It's the middle of the night, and we can be quick about it. They have posted only two guards. Some of us can set up a diversion while the others cut down the body. This is something we must do. They have disgraced the Prince and the King!"

A long moment of silence was my only answer. I moved toward the door hoping at least some of the men would follow—some did.

William, Rob, Barrett, and I stealthily moved from street to street, making our way toward the square. The others stayed behind.

"How are we going to do this with only four of us, Cedric?" whispered William as we crossed our last street before reaching the square.

"I'm not sure, William," I whispered back. "Let's take a look at the square from behind that brick wall by those trees. We'll form a plan from there."

We moved carefully to the low brick wall. Our backs were completely covered by the thick trees on one side, and the brick wall protected the other. From this vantage point, we could easily see the entire square, including the large oak tree in the center, thanks to the light of a half moon.

Something was wrong!

My eyes were fully adjusted to the dim light, but I could not see the body of the Prince. I forced my eyes to decipher what must be an illusion caused by shadows. As I focused more carefully, I could even see the rope. His body was gone!

"What did they do with his body?" I turned and asked the other three.

"I don't know," said Barrett. "But look on the ground beneath the tree. The guards are either asleep or are knocked out cold."

"I don't like this, Cedric," said Rob. "Let's get out of here before we're found out and hanged ourselves."

At that moment, we froze and our hearts nearly stopped beating. Just a few feet away, on the other side of the brick wall, stood a large man. In our earnest desire to see what happened at the oak tree, this fellow must have quietly made his way to our cover and now was upon us.

"Why do you look for the Prince here?" spoke the man in a thick accent I'd never heard before.

"We came to bury the body," I said. "Can you tell us where they've taken the body, sir? Where is the Prince?"

The large fellow gave a slight chuckle. "Do not worry, the Prince will find you!" he said.

With the speed of a cat, his large form jumped the brick wall and disappeared into the shadows of some trees. I thought I heard a scrape of steel on brick as he crossed the wall. He was gone as quickly as he appeared.

"What is that supposed to mean?" asked William in a hushed voice.

"I don't know, William," I said. "But I agree with Rob. It's time to leave this place. Let's get back to Barrett's shop."

"What do you mean someone's taken the body?" asked Jonathan, one of the other knights in Barrett's back room. "Surely it must have been the Noble

Knights. No one is foolish enough to try such a risky task, present company excluded of course."

"Look, if it were the Noble Knights, then why were there two guards sleeping beneath an empty oak tree in the middle of the square?" asked Rob. "The guards must have been overtaken and knocked out. Then someone took the body. I don't know why, but maybe it was the large fellow that nearly scared us out of our wits."

"What large fellow are you talking about?" asked a fellow knight.

"Just as we were getting ready to leave, a large—," I stopped mid-sentence.

There were footsteps approaching outside from the back of Barrett's shop. We all instinctively grabbed for our swords.

"Someone must have followed you," whispered Jonathan.

The footsteps grew louder. We stared at the back door. There were at least six men by the sound of the boots on the cobblestone. We braced ourselves for a deadly fight that surely would come from the Noble Knights. The men walked to our door...and passed. We all breathed a sigh of relief and relaxed our swords.

"Greetings, gentlemen!" A voice not of our own spoke from behind us yet in the same room. All of our attention had been on the back door while someone else obviously gained entrance from the front.

I dared not turn to see the owner of the voice. It was familiar, too familiar. The hair on my arms and neck stood straight, manifesting the near terror I felt. I could tell the others felt it too. I did not fear the voice but what the voice meant. *I must be going mad*, I thought.

Slowly I turned, my eyes leading the way. Once I saw the author of those words, I stumbled back, catching myself on a center support beam. There were no words on my tongue or coherent thoughts in my mind, just simple shock. Before us stood—the Prince!

Some of the knights stumbled into chairs, while others grabbed something to keep themselves from falling. Two were making their way toward the back door.

I saw the scars on his body, but his strength and power were even more accentuated now.

"Do not be afraid, my friends," spoke the Prince again. "I am not a ghost, and you are not going mad. Please sit down and let me explain."

"M-My Lord," I stumbled on my words, "how can this be? I saw you die. I saw you hang on the tree. What trick or miracle is this?"

"A trick it is not, my dear Cedric," said the Prince. "But miracle, ah, yes. You see, gentlemen, my Father is not only wise and wealthy, but he also commands power that none here can comprehend. The Noble Knights will not believe though they see me with their own eyes. That is why my Father sent me here to train you. You are privileged, my friends. You are part of the plan to restore his kingdom."

Slowly we came to believe that what we saw was not an apparition but truly the Prince we'd grown to love and serve. Terror and shock were eventually replaced by joy and excitement.

"Now you can help us defeat this evil Kifus and the Noble Knights, my Lord?" asked Rob.

"No, Rob," said the Prince. "I must return to my Father's kingdom, and you will not fight Kifus and the Noble Knights."

"Then what is this all for, my Lord?" asked William.

"You must remember what I taught you and why I taught you. Your battle is with the greater foe, the Dark Knight. Do not be fooled. He also has powers that will amaze and trick many people. You must stay strong and wary. He knows I have trained you, and he will seek to destroy you before I can return. You must add to the Knights of the Prince. Be vigilant in your training, and above all, stay true to the Code. I was your example. Now you must be the example to others!"

Those same compassionate eyes took each of us in; the eyes that burned like fire.

"Why must you leave us again, my Prince?" I asked painfully. I did not share the Prince's confidence in us.

"Cedric, your heart is strong in the Code. Trust in it and in me. As long as you live by the Code, I will be with you. What I have taught you will not fail you. I go to prepare our kingdom across the sea for the battle that must come with the Dark Knight and his Shadow Warriors. Do not be afraid. I will come back for you."

I looked at the strong face of the Prince and found my hope again.

"Your sword is here, my Prince," I said. I retrieved it from the same chest that Leinad had stored it in for so many years. I opened the cloth that held his glorious sword.

"It found me in my despair," I said and held it before the Prince.

He smiled and lifted it from my hands. "Do not forget, my friends. It is the Code that makes the sword worth carrying."

We all knelt before him, and then bid farewell. I was lonely again, but this time, I knew it would not last forever.

Chapter 10 - "We Build"

At first we worked in secret, quietly adding strength and numbers to the Knights of the Prince. But soon our confidence with the sword and our belief in the King, the Prince, and the Code drove us to recruit openly. Anyone who believed our story of the Prince and had a heart to follow the Code was welcomed and trained.

The Noble Knights hated us as they hated the Prince. We were hunted but not defeated. The Prince had taught us well, and the Noble Knights soon realized that we were not going away. Small battles broke out across the country, but the Knights of the Prince stood strong. Some of our men were beaten and thrown into prison, but this only solidified our resolve to accomplish our mission—be ready for the Prince when he returns, and be prepared for the great battle with the Dark Knight.

"Are you ready, my brother?" I asked William. The Code made friends of strangers and brothers of friends. William and I were now kindred spirits, not of our own doing, but because of what the Prince taught us to believe in.

"Yes, Cedric, let's be on our way," said William. "The road is long before us, and we must make Chandril before sundown."

We set off on our journey that morning hoping to find more recruits in the neighboring city of Chandril. Along the way, we came across a man and his family journeying to our own city of Chessington. A wheel on his cart was broken, and we stopped to help. We told them of our mission and shared the story of the Prince. Their ears yearned to hear of such hope and promise.

"Please be careful in Chandril," said the man as we completed the work on his cart. "Not only is there poverty in the city, but also many of the people have become bitter and hateful. There are evil men that have great influence over the people. It is not a safe place anymore. That is why I am taking my family to Chessington."

"Find the shop owned by a man named Barrett," I said to the man. "Tell him William and Cedric sent you. He will help you get settled and provide protection for your family."

"Thank you for all you have done, gentlemen," replied the man. His wife smiled gratefully as they passed and proceeded on toward Chessington.

The delay caused us to arrive in Chandril at dusk. I felt the city's oppression in my spirit as we entered the outskirts. We walked up a broad street where shops were closing windows and locking doors at the end of a day's work. Our presence caught the stares from many weary faces. We stopped one fellow as he began to shut his door.

"Good sir, would you be kind enough to direct us toward the nearest inn?" William asked.

He glanced at our tunics and saw the emblem of the Prince. His face revealed his disgust.

"I have heard of your kind and your lies. Stay away from my shop!" came his sharp reply as he slammed the door in our faces.

A gang of six burly men across the street turned their attention to us when they heard the door slam. We walked on our way but were acutely aware of the menacing men following our every turn. They quickened their pace to gain ground. Finally, we could not ignore them any longer and turned to face them. The shops had all closed by now, and the sun was set. The residual light from horizon clouds still illuminated the city enough for us to see that the faces of these men were not friendly. The six figures slowly surrounded us, each brandishing a sword on his hip. Timid faces appeared in the windows of the nearby shops and homes.

"Can we help you, gentlemen?" I asked while searching their faces for intent. William watched their swords closely.

"Who are you?" asked the lead brute.

"We are from Chessington and are looking for a place to stay," I replied.

"I didn't ask where you were from," came his brusque reply. "I recognize that mark, and it is not welcome here. You should be more careful about where you walk."

"You have allegiance to the Noble Knights then?" I asked.

"We have allegiance to no one but ourselves," growled the man. "Kill them and take their money," he ordered his men. They all drew their swords and advanced on us.

We drew our swords quickly and positioned ourselves against the wall of the shop behind us. The situation was not good. Even if they were only average swordsmen, their numbers would soon overwhelm us.

They attacked with fury; William and I found ourselves in a fight for our lives. Our swords collided, but there were too many. I injured one with a quick slice from my right, but then I caught a thrust through my left arm. The steel burned as it entered and left my flesh. I heard William gasp in pain as he caught a slice across his chest that bled profusely. He recovered and brought down his attacker with a quick thrust to his opponent's abdomen. The leader filled his place. Our situation was hopeless and death was near.

My thoughts turned to the Prince. *Would his work here carry on effectively without us? Had we let him down?*

From within my heart came my final words to the world. I shouted for all to hear, "The King reigns—and his Son!"

At that moment, time and movement seemed to slow down. Just when all seemed lost, something astonishing happened. From above our heads came the sound of deliverance. A man jumped from the roof and landed just behind the ring of attacking brutes. From between the buildings to my left came another man that positioned himself beside the first. The band of thieves was as shocked as we, and the fighting momentarily stopped. The two men held brilliant swords, and they themselves were massive men of power. Their chiseled facial features matched their muscular frames, which were partially hidden by peasant clothes. They were...Silent Warriors!

William collapsed from the loss of blood, and I moved to cover his position. The Silent Warriors advanced on the thieves without hesitation. There was no mercy. In less than a minute, four of the thieves were prone on the ground, and the remaining two managed to escape down an alleyway.

The Silent Warriors wiped their swords and sheathed them. One knelt down and lifted William with the ease of a parent lifting his child.

"I am Keef, and this is Ramon," spoke the other knight. "Follow me."

Keef led us to an old building near the southern part of Chandril. Once inside, Ramon laid William on a table and tore off a portion of his own tunic to dress the wound. William was still unconscious.

"Thank you for saving our lives," I said to them both. "Is William…?"

"William will live," spoke Keef. "Ramon will make sure of it." It was almost an order, but Ramon nodded in agreement. I felt some relief in their confidence.

"How did you know to come to our aid?" I asked Keef.

"You spoke the words of the Prince, and your situation was desperate. Only then are we allowed to reveal ourselves," said Keef.

I had forgotten what the Prince told us and felt stupid. My foolishness nearly cost William his life.

"Is there any message from the Prince?" I asked hopefully. It had been many months since he left us to return to the King.

"We have not been home for a long time," said Keef. He began dressing my upper arm through which I'd been pierced. "There is no message, but do not lose heart. Continue to build. What you tasted tonight is the work of the Dark Knight. These people do not swear allegiance to anyone. Therefore, they become his tools to work anarchy in the kingdom. When the time is right, he will sweep in and bring tyrannical rule, which the people will gladly swallow for the sake of order. The

Dark Knight and his Shadow Warriors are moving, and you must be vigilant."

I watched Ramon cover William's gash with a salve from his own pouch. The sweet odor of the salve filled the small room.

I turned back toward Keef. "Where did the Dark Knight come from, and why is he such a fierce enemy of the King?" I asked.

Keef finished bandaging my wound and sat down on a wooden stool. He leaned against the wall and folded one arm over his thick chest while his other hand stroked his cheek. I saw a flood of memories pass over his thoughts. I was ready to hear a story that might make sense of this strange saga.

Chapter 11 - "Origins of Evil"

"**R**amon and I were both there," began Keef, "many, many years ago." Keef was clearly a veteran of warfare. His dark blue eyes conveyed a "serious business" attitude in all that he did. His hair was sand colored and cut short. He owned a square jaw that matched his determination. His broad neck, shoulders, and arms revealed tremendous strength and terminated in hands that dwarfed my own. Yes, Keef would make a most formidable foe. I was glad to be on the same side.

Ramon finished dressing William's wound and joined us on another stool. Ramon was just as large as Keef with slightly darker skin and hair. He was obviously a man of action and very few words.

Keef continued. "In our kingdom across the sea, life was peaceful, and the Dark Knight was not always our enemy. In fact, he was the head of the Silent Warriors. There were nearly five thousand of us. We followed his orders without question. He proved himself to be the best of the best and won favor with the King. His given name is Lucius. Next to the King and his Son, no one had more authority or power than Lucius.

"I don't understand," I said. "What happened to make Lucius the King's arch enemy?"

Keef hesitated as he pondered his memories. "I'm not sure, Cedric. You have lived with the Prince and know that there is only kindness and compassion in his heart. I believe the only reason Lucius eventually turned on the Prince was because of pure jealousy. I am sure that his pride in his own ability, and pride in his power, ultimately led to his downfall. I first noticed it during our drills. One day, the Prince came to check on us as Lucius led us through the training. When the Prince approached, Lucius bowed but not in heart. I sensed the slightest hint of contempt. And when the Prince left us, Lucius watched him carefully; his thoughts were clearly elsewhere. I was not the only knight that noticed. Most of us questioned our own judgment, yet some seemed interested in Lucius' new-found spirit of arrogance."

"As the weeks wore on, Lucius grew more and more rebellious in front of the knights and yet hid it from the Prince and the King. One of the knights approached him on his attitude. Lucius pulled him aside and spoke but a few brief words to the knight. We saw fear on the knight's face, and he was silent from then on. None of us dared challenge Lucius, for there was none that could defeat him. However, a commander's heart is not his own. I felt the disdain and rebellious attitudes filtering down the ranks. Many of the knights were clearly more loyal to Lucius than to the King and the Prince. Risking our lives at the hand of Lucius, Ramon and I decided to take the matter to the Prince."

William moaned on the table as he stirred. Ramon and I walked over to check on him, but he fell back asleep. As I returned to my stool to hear the rest of Keef's story, I became acutely aware of my hunger. We had not eaten supper since arriving in Chandril, and all of the activity eliminated any opportunity to eat. I grabbed the bread and cheese and offered some to the Silent Warriors. They accepted graciously. I waited patiently for the rest of Keef's story, pondering all that he had told me already. Keef finished his food and drank heavily from his water flask. He leaned back on his stool and continued.

"Ramon and I agreed to approach the King's palace at night so as not to draw attention to ourselves. Even at night, the palace is more glorious than anything I have ever seen. You and William will see it one day, Cedric. All of the Knights of the Prince will see it."

"As we came to the palace, four other knights intercepted us. We greeted them and tried to pass on nonchalantly, but they would not give way. It was only then that I realized just how serious the situation had become. We were men sworn to the King. We trained and fought side by side and even ate our meals together. We wore the same emblem, but these four had changed their allegiance. The realization of their actions shocked me. We tried to appeal to their sworn loyalty, but it was clear these men had crossed the line in their minds and were now doing so in a physical way. They threatened to kill us if we would not join them. For the first time in the history of the King's kingdom, two swords of the Silent Warriors met as enemies…a rebellion was born."

"We fought defensively at first, still not wanting to believe what was happening. But when they drew first blood on Ramon, we knew there was no turning back."

Ramon lifted the portion of his tunic that remained, after using part of it for William's bandage, and revealed a deep scar that crossed his chest.

Keef continued. "Ramon quickly recovered and slew his attacker. I injured a second to make the fight even, but our skirmish brought attention and three more knights came to join the fight. I recognized them and guessed them to be loyal to Lucius—I was right. Our situation was grave. We fought back to back to provide as much protection for each other as possible, but we could not last long."

Keef's eyes narrowed and his brows furrowed. I sympathized with him, having just escaped our own deaths by a very narrow margin. It is a hopeless, ugly situation to be in.

"I was never so glad to see the Prince ride up on his white stallion as I was that night. The five traitorous knights ran to the shadows and disappeared. Their rebellion boldness temporarily faded in the presence of the Prince. We explained our understanding of the situation to the Prince as we walked with him to the palace."

"'Come with me to the King,' said the Prince. Micalem joined us inside the palace. Micalem was second in command under Lucius and was a brilliant knight as well as an outstanding warrior. His face revealed his sorrow at the news of the rebellion. The three of us and the Prince entered the throne room and approached the King."

"We knelt before his Majesty, and he bid us to rise. 'It has happened, Father,' spoke the Prince. 'Yes, as I feared it would,' said the King. 'Gather the Silent Warriors that are loyal and prepare for war, my Son.' 'As you wish, Father,' replied the Prince."

"We bowed and left the King. The Prince took us to another chamber. 'Micalem,' he said. 'You are now in command of the Silent Warriors. Stay with me to plan our next move. Keef and Ramon, gather those you know to be loyal and brief them on the situation. Then spread out and gather all other loyal knights. Gentlemen, there is no war more deadly nor devastating than a war from within. Be careful.'"

"We turned to leave. 'Keef, Ramon,' said the Prince, 'well done!' 'Well done' was all that the Prince said, and it was all I needed to take on an army. When we go back home, those are the words I hope to hear again."

"We gathered our men through the night, and by morning the lines were drawn. Lucius had claimed over fifteen hundred knights. Some of our finest warriors had sided with Lucius—men like Envor, Hatlin, and Luskan. Knights we had respected and admired were now our enemies. I still don't understand how Lucius convinced them to turn against the King!"

"The war was fierce, but we outnumbered them two to one. Their only option was to flee the kingdom or be destroyed. And that, Sir Cedric, is why this land is in peril. The Dark Knight brought his Shadow Warriors, as they became known, to this kingdom. Although it is the King's, the Dark Knight is determined to rule it. And if he can't rule it, he will destroy it. You may never have seen the Dark Knight, but you can be sure he is here. Even the Silent Warriors fear his fight, for he is powerful and merciless. Only the Prince himself is able to overcome him."

"That explains a lot, Keef," I said. "But why did the Prince come here disguised as a peasant? Why not just bring an entire army and retake the kingdom?"

"Because he doesn't just want a kingdom, Cedric," replied Keef. "He wants a kingdom of people with hearts that love and serve willingly...people like you. He wants people that honestly desire to follow the Code. A full-scale assault on this land would destroy that. The

King loves these people, and he has provided a way for them to live."

"The Prince made a way, didn't he?" I asked.

"That's right," said Keef. "I remember the day when the King told us of his plan to save this land. We could not believe he would jeopardize his own son to save this kingdom. At first we thought it was foolish, but soon we realized it was pure love—love for the people. The Prince understood, and we knew that he was the only one capable of being successful. We were all at the palace to bid him farewell. He came from the inner court, and we all knelt before him. Thousands of knights in shining armor knelt before the Prince who was dressed in dirty rags. But those clothes couldn't hide the splendor of his character, as you saw."

"Yes, Keef," I said. "There was something about that man!"

Keef continued. "We rose and saluted the Prince with drawn swords as he passed between our lines. When he neared the gates, the King walked to his Son and embraced him. I saw a tear fall from the King's cheek and moisten the beautiful stones at their feet. Then he left. We tried to provide an escort, but he refused. He took no weapon, not even a sword. He said he would live as the people do for a time, and he limited our mission while he was here."

Keef's story provided many answers, but there was still one question to ask. "The Dark Knight must have known that the Prince was in the kingdom," I said, finding affirmation in a nod from Keef. "Why didn't the Dark Knight attempt to kill the Prince before he had a chance to train and to build up our forces?"

Keef leaned forward, rested his left elbow on his knee, and placed his right hand on the other knee. His eyes sparkled as though he was anxious to answer.

"He did, Cedric!" I could tell that this was a part of the story Keef was hoping to tell.

"Do you remember the last time you and William visited Leinad?" Keef asked.

"Yes," I said. "It was just a few days before the Prince revealed himself as the King's son in the square."

"That's right," Keef replied. "Later that day, the Prince, Ramon, and I visited Leinad too. He had kept the sword of the Prince for years—waiting for the day to give it to him. That was the day—the day when the 'one who is worthy' would carry the sword and deliver the people...deliver the kingdom!"

"When we entered his home, Leinad came and stood before the Prince. He looked into the eyes of the King's Son, then reached forth and placed his hand on the Prince's chest. I could see the burden of fifty years leave his face. 'Now I rest, for the mighty arm of the King has arrived!' said Leinad, and he knelt before the Prince. 'You are a true and faithful knight, Sir Leinad,' spoke the Prince. He helped Leinad to his feet. 'Please bring the chest,' asked Leinad of Ramon and me. We retrieved the old wooden chest from the corner, placed it at his feet, and opened it for him. He carefully unfolded the cloth that was wrapped about the sword and reverently lifted it to the Prince. 'Only one is worthy,' said Leinad as the Prince placed his hand about the hilt of the beautiful sword. The Master was ready to fulfill the purpose of the existence of this magnificent sword. The Prince raised the sword before him and proclaimed, 'Now is the time...let it begin!'"

"At the command of the Prince, two other Silent Warriors escorted Leinad to a ship that awaited to take him to the kingdom across the sea. His mission was complete, and the King had called him home."

"From Leinad's home, we followed the Prince deep into the country on horseback. The Dark Knight knew that he would rule this kingdom forever if he could destroy the Prince. Thus...the challenge."

Keef paused, gathering details in his mind.

"What was the challenge?" I asked, too impatient to wait for him to continue on his own.

After another moment of thoughtful silence, Keef continued. "The Dark Knight challenged the Prince to one single duel, hoping to kill the Prince and end his mission before it began. The Prince accepted because he knew it was his final preparation for the monumental task that was before him. Defeating the Dark Knight would confirm him as the only true authority in Arrethtrae."

"On the crest of a hill near the base of the Northern Mountains, we joined with two hundred mounted Silent Warriors. Apprehension hung in the air. Across a span of rugged terrain, many of the Dark Knight's Shadow Warriors lined the horizon. The Prince rode before our solemn line. 'This is neither the time nor the place for battle,' he said for all to hear. 'This fight is for me alone!'"

"The Prince rode to meet Lucius midway. As the distance between the champion of darkness and the champion of light closed, a silence fell upon the countryside. Even the birds stopped their song. It was as though nature itself recognized the potential peril of the land. Dark clouds had rolled in and obscured the sun, but now the air was silent—a calm before the storm. I remember thinking how ironic it was that the fate of all the people of Arrethtrae would ride on the outcome of this single fight, and they were completely ignorant of its happening."

"With only a few strides between them, Lucius and the Prince dismounted and drew their swords. The ultimate battle between the two best swordsmen that ever lived was about to begin—hatred versus love—bondage versus freedom—the Dark Knight versus the Prince. The future of Arrethtrae was unfolding at this very moment in time."

"They slowly circled each other at a safe distance, calculating and planning their strategies—feeling the terrain, anticipating strengths, looking for weaknesses. The silence of the countryside gave way to an eerie, low growl that built in strength and emanated from the unified voices of the Shadow Warriors. It was a taunting war cry of a vicious enemy that was heightened by the distant thunder of storm clouds. Micalem was first to respond. 'Honor...Glory...Power...The Prince!' he shouted. 'Honor...Glory...Power...The Prince!' The chant flowed down our line until the words resonated off the hillsides and mixed with the opposing growl in a bizarre and unnatural song. The rhythm and intensity increased with the roar and flash of lightening—all in anticipation of the first strike."

"Lucius and the Prince simultaneously positioned themselves and readied their swords. It was Lucius that struck first, and both lines of warriors yielded to silent observation as the fight ensued. Lucius engaged with a quick combination, and the Prince met each stroke with precision. The initial engagements were sporadic as they felt for each other's ability. I realized that my own heart was pounding and my muscles were strained. I tried to relax, but could not; too much was at stake. The fight quickly developed into a ferocious volley of cuts, slices, and thrusts. The steel of their blades screamed through the air unceasingly. Two unyielding masters were in a battle to the death. Lucius attacked with the speed of a viper, and the Prince countered with the power of a lion."

Keef leaned back and drew in a deep breath. "I am a warrior well acquainted with battle, Cedric. But I must admit that the intensity of that duel between Lucius and the Prince made it frightening to watch."

I glanced at Ramon. His eyes were shut, and a nearly imperceptible nod affirmed Keef's feeling of unease during the fight.

"At one point in the fight, Lucius aggressively advanced with a quick series of combinations that caused the Prince to move back. His foot caught on a stone behind him, and he fell. Lucius knew it was his chance to end the fight and instantly brought down a powerful vertical cut on the Prince. Flat on his back, and with no time or place to move, the Prince executed a quick parry that deflected Lucius' blade. The sword tore into the ground to the left of the Prince's shoulder. The Prince rolled to his right and onto his knees, but the maneuver momentary exposed his back to his enemy. Anticipating Lucius' next move, the Prince swiftly locked his sword above his head and caught Lucius' next vertical cut. The Prince simultaneously rotated on one knee and exploded a horizontal slice that moved at blinding speed full circle around to Lucius. Realizing that his sword was incapable of making the distance to counter the oncoming slice, Lucius jumped back as the tip of the Prince's sword grazed his chest. This gave the Prince enough time to recover and reestablish his position. I heard Lucius curse—the Prince had thwarted his perfect opportunity."

"The thunderstorm was now upon us, and day turned to night. The lightening flashed from cloud to cloud, and the ground shook with the roar of the thunder. Our horses pawed the ground nervously. Lucius advanced again. His fight teetered on the edge of 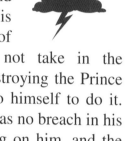 recklessness—taking risks he did not take in the beginning. He was obsessed with destroying the Prince and was willing to sacrifice injury to himself to do it. But the Prince stood firm, and there was no breach in his defense. Lucius' ferocity was wearing on him, and the fight began to tilt. The Prince advanced with such power and speed that Lucius found himself in methodic retreat. The sky began to unload its burden of water in a steady rain that soaked my clothes instantly."

"Lucius attempted a more offensive posture, but the Prince was now in control, and Lucius knew it. The Prince paused and stared at his archenemy. The scowl on Lucius' face revealed his hatred for this enemy and also his understanding that the future of Arrethtrae belonged to the Prince!"

"The Prince advanced with combinations and maneuvers I had never seen before. His dominance over Lucius was unbelievable! It was time for the end, and the Prince brought forth a sequence of cuts that nearly paralyzed Lucius. One massive blow caused Lucius to lose his balance and his sword. The grisly weapon of the Dark Knight was finally still, and Lucius lay prone before the Prince. The entire line of Silent Warriors cheered in victory. The Prince glared at this enemy of two kingdoms and spoke. 'My Father loved you, and you spurned his love. He has postponed your judgment for now. Your final destruction is yet before you, but it *is* a certainty!'"

"The Prince withdrew and mounted his stallion. We rode to a distant camp. He was tired, and we guarded him while he ate and slept. Two days later, you saw him in the square. From that day on, our involvement in his mission was extremely limited. It was hard not to be by his side. When they took him to the tree, there were a thousand Silent Warriors ready to wipe out the entire city, but he forbade us. He did it for you, Cedric. He did it for all of the people who will follow him."

My eyes filled with tears again as I remembered that day in the square. How could anyone care that much for me?

There was a long silence before Ramon spoke. "It is time to leave, Keef."

"Yes, Ramon," said Keef. "I suppose you are right. Take care, Cedric. And remember, the story did not end at the tree. For you and your people, that is where the story begins."

"Thank you, Keef," I said. "Thank you, Ramon. I will not forget you. May we meet again someday!"

"We will, Cedric," replied Keef. "We will!"
And with that, they donned their crude cloaks again and entered the streets.

As the door closed, William stirred and awoke. "Lie still, brother," I said.

"Where are we, Cedric?" asked William. "I thought we were going to die. What happened?"

I chuckled. "William, I don't think you're going to believe me, but I'll give it a try anyway."

Chapter 12 - "Night of Knights"

The Knights of the Prince grew tremendously in numbers, and the anarchy of the kingdom seemed to match our pace. The kingdom of Arrethtrae was on the verge of self-destruction like a volcano ready to erupt. We built and strengthened, but the Dark Knight countered with discord and chaos.

We sent recruiters for the Prince to every city in the kingdom. We worked hard for years, and eventually everyone, men, women, and children alike, heard the story of the Prince and was given an opportunity to join us.

Our beloved city of Chessington seemed to be the Dark Knight's focus. We began seeing more and more of the Shadow Warriors. They were disguised as commoners, but we could tell they were much more than that. The Noble Knights faded into history and either gave way or were absorbed into a new form of government. The city chose a strong man by the name of Alexander Histen as its governor. Strong is a broad description of Governor Histen. It applies to his physical strength as well as his political strength. His charisma seemed to magnetize the people to his cause. I did not like him nor was I fooled by his sweet rhetoric. As chaos increased, so did his control over the people. It was "necessary," so Governor Histen said, "to maintain security and peace in the city." He smoothly convinced the people it was for their own good. The desperate citizens swallowed it all, for they had no choice. In the back of my mind, I wondered how much of the chaos was generated by Histen himself. It was just as Keef told me.

Over the next year, Alexander Histen widened his sphere of influence to include most of the surrounding cities and villages. It was at this time that serious persecution returned. Histen scoffed at our story of the return of the Prince and denied the King's authority in the land altogether. He labeled us as haters of peace and harmony, the very antithesis of what we were. His propaganda worked, and our mission became much more difficult. Many of the Knights of the Prince were beaten and imprisoned for the crime of causing disturbance in the city. My own scars testify to such atrocities. In spite of this, we still found people hungry for hope. They yearned for hope in truth and peace with freedom as a companion, for the peace they tasted now was falsely induced under tyrannical rule. Eventually, Histen changed his title to "Governor Supreme." It was clear to us that Alexander Histen cared for only one thing—total control of the entire kingdom. During these difficult times, it was our belief in the Code that kept us together.

"How long will this go on, Cedric," asked William as we walked toward the meeting place. Barrett's shop was discovered and burned some time ago. We found a safer place for him and his family on the outskirts of the city, but our new meeting place was still in the heart of the city to allow easy travel for all knights.

"It does seem nearly impossible to continue, doesn't it, William," I replied. "It's been so long since the Prince left us, and yet I know he will be true to his word and deliver us from this bondage."

The moonlight lit our path, and we moved carefully down the streets and alleys, ever vigilant to watch all sides.

"Ironic isn't it, Cedric," said William quietly. "When we first met the Prince, we felt we were in bondage to the poverty, but now we know what true bondage is. I don't see any end to Histen's desire for power and total control of the people."

We turned onto another alley and began walking down it.

"Nor do I, Will—," I stopped mid sentence and we both took cover in the shadows. Other men occupied the alley already. We were not seen, for they too were deep in conversation and walking our way.

They paused some fifty feet away. Both men were broad and tall. I had never seen either one before, but I recognized their posture. Fear began to grip my heart, and I fought to maintain control of it. Though they were dressed in common clothes, these men were knights! I knew they were either Silent Warriors or Shadow Warriors. William and I froze in the shadows and strained to hear their conversation. They spoke softly, but their deep voices carried far enough for us to hear.

"—nearly complete with his preparation plans in the North," said the first figure.

"How is Kelson doing in the South? We must be ready in all quadrants or the mission will be delayed. Time is short," said the second figure.

"He is nearly ready but I must tell you that—"

CRASH! A door beside the two figures burst open, and a huge menacing man lunged toward the two figures with sword drawn. Across the alley, two more monstrous men flew toward the same two figures, each flashing a wicked looking sword.

In the blink of an eye, the two figures had thrown back their cloaks and drawn their swords. Back to back, they faced their enemies. In an instant, we became enlightened to the situation. The two figures we first heard talking had the look of serious determination, but there was not the look of hate in their countenance like there was on their three attackers. The attackers were warriors belonging to the Dark Knight...Shadow Warriors! The first two men were the Prince's Silent Warriors.

The swords flew at blinding speed. We heard a thunderous and continuous clash of steel upon steel. I had seen the skill of a Silent Warrior against mere men, and I had fought against a Shadow Warrior first hand, but never before had I seen two such formidable forces meet face to face. The fight raged on in a flurry of slices, cuts, and thrusts—a precise picture of good versus evil.

"William," I whispered. "We must help them!"

"I am ready, Cedric," came his reply.

Though my stomach rose to my throat, we drew our swords and ran toward the battle. The five warriors heard us approach but did not know upon which side we would join.

"For the Prince!" shouted William.

At those words, one of the Shadow Warriors left his fight and lunged toward us with renewed hatred and anger burning in his eyes.

William and I traded offensive and defensive posturing to keep the Shadow Warrior distracted. Our past encounters with the Shadow Warriors over the last few years had taught us a great deal, and we had grown in strength, skill, and experience. William defended against a combination, and I saw an opportunity, which I took. The Shadow Warrior screamed a curse at me as my sword passed under his left arm and separated the flesh beneath his ribs. He charged me with a full force blow that sent me stumbling. He seized the momentary break in our fight to escape between two buildings, clutching his side as he went. We moved toward the other fight, but these Shadow Warriors, seeing their disadvantage, also took flight. All of us scanned the area for further threat, but found none.

After a moment of silence, interrupted only by heavy breathing, swords were sheathed.

"Thank you for your help," said one of the Silent Warriors. "Normally we avoid such confrontations, but lately it has not been possible. Their presence here is growing quickly."

"Yes, we've noticed as well," I said. "What does it mean?"

He searched my face with narrow eyes. "You are Cedric?" he asked.

"I am," I replied. "And this is William."

"We must go. Time is short, very short. Tell your people to be ready!"

He nodded to his companion toward one side of the alley, and together they left us quickly and quietly.

"Be ready for what?" I asked, but there was no one to answer.

Chapter 13 - "Change of Heart"

Over the next three days, we spread the message from the Silent Warrior to the Knights of the Prince. "Be ready!"

Of course everyone repeated my question, "Be ready for what?" Before we discovered the answer, the kingdom of Arrethtrae saw the dawn of total oppression.

I awoke to a morning that was bright and cool, yet I felt a heavy darkness descend like a thick fog. I attributed it to a restless night's sleep and tried to shake it off as I washed my face in cool water, but it lingered.

Rob, William, and I journeyed to Northern Chessington to organize a mission beyond our region. The city of Drisdol was in desperate need of supplies. Those who pledged allegiance to the Prince were plundered daily by Histen's men. Though we suffered similar persecution here in Chessington, our city was larger and afforded greater protection and supplies.

For several streets, we walked vigilant and in silence. It was William that spoke first. "There is evil in the city today."

"I feel it too, William," replied Rob. His ever-present grin was absent. "We've done all we can to recruit people for the Prince. Our numbers are great, but Histen's oppression and control increase with each passing day. How long must we carry on? Why must we carry on?"

I felt Rob's despair and was also growing weary of the fight. Our brothers and sisters were persecuted continuously. Histen wanted us out of his way, and I knew that persecution would soon turn to killing. Yet the Prince was—

"Get your grimy paws off my fruit you filthy lit'l mutt." The shouts of a produce shop owner interrupted my thoughts. A young boy scampered over a barrel and knocked down the shop owner's fruit and vegetable stand. The boy ran across the street with a stolen apple in hand. We winced at the string of cursing that followed. The shop owner's face was red with rage, and he emphasized each curse with a clenched fist.

The curses eventually subsided until he turned to see his produce scattered on the walk and the street.

"May we help you, sir?" I asked as politely as possible, hoping to soothe his anger a bit.

The man was barrel-chested with stocky legs to match. He looked middle-aged and his curly, dark hair was laced with wisps of gray. He glanced our way, but his countenance had not changed. The anger in his face seemed to be a steady companion to him.

"You stay away from my food," he bellowed. "I'm no fool to trust the likes of you nor any other thief in this city."

He yelled over his shoulder toward the shop door. "Cassy! Get out here an' clean this mess up, right now!"

Within seconds, a woman, who appeared to be his wife, emerged. I could see her beauty beneath the lines of strife and the bruises of abuse. She did not look up at us but quickly moved toward the spill, taking care not to get too close to her husband. His lingering anger was still evident though. He raised his hand to strike and vent his frustration as she passed.

"I would advise you not to do that, sir," declared William as we stepped forward.

Somewhat surprised, the man turned to look at us. "I will do as I please, and you will stay out of my business!" It was enough distraction for his wife to pass by and beyond his reach. The moment passed, and he cursed at us as he turned to right the fruit and vegetable stand.

Rob's face displayed the anger we all felt as we stepped into the street to pass this shop of despair. A few steps brought us to the man's wife, and we knelt to help her fill a basket.

"Please—no!" came a soft plea from her weathered lips. "Just leave now or he will hurt me more."

The man was kneeling and reaching for a broken table leg on the ground near the base of his shop's front wall when he glanced up to see us giving aid to his wife. "You get your—Aaah!"

His scream was one of searing pain. He stood up to reveal his demise. A fire asp had bitten him and was coiled around his forearm.

The fire asp is not only the deadliest snake in the kingdom, but its effects on its victim are horrific. The poison is quick, and death is certain once it reaches the brain. Its length is about that of a man's foot, and its breadth is no bigger around than a finger. It is brown in color making it difficult to see until it strikes, at which time the skin of the asp changes color to a fiery red. It is aggressive and bites only once. It then dies with its victim. On first strike, it sinks its fangs deep into the skin while simultaneously coiling around the victim to empty its deadly poison.

The initial sensation around the bite is a torturous burning and swelling that spreads with the poison until the entire body is absorbed in searing hot pain. As the poison enters the brain, the overwhelming pain drives the victim into madness. Death follows within moments of the initial bite.

The shop owner continued to scream in pain as he clutched his right arm with his left hand—panic was evident on his face.

"William! Rob! Quick—come with me," I shouted. We ran to the man and sat him on the ground. "William, remove the asp with your knife. Rob, give him something to bite on and hold his arm steady!" I ordered, knowing we had only seconds before it was too late.

The man's wife slowly stood up and backed into the shop. Her mouth was open and shock was on her face.

"Stay as calm as you can, sir. The slower your heart beats, the better chance we have of saving your life," I said as gently as possible.

My grandfather once saved his brother from the poisonous bite of a fire asp, but the odds were slim. I had never heard of any other victim living through the ordeal.

I secured a leather strap around the man's upper arm and tightened it until no blood could flow in either direction. William finished removing the asp. It lay limp and lifeless on the walk, but its poison was ravaging the man's arm and spreading quickly. The swelling was already spreading to his hand and to his upper arm. So was the pain. His legs shook violently, and the cloth between his teeth only slightly muffled his screams.

"William, quickly make some mud from the alley and bring it here," I said.

I unsheathed my knife and opened a vein above and below the bite on his arm to spill the contaminated blood. I massaged his arm toward the cuts to empty the veins. I knew he might lose his arm, but it was his only hope. William returned with the mud.

"We must prick his arm in sixty places before we apply the mud," I told William. Rob was completely occupied holding down the man's other arm. I glanced at the man's shoulder to see if the poison had spread beyond my leather strap and was slightly relieved to see no evidence of swelling there. The small cuts we gave him hardly bled—a good sign. We quickly encased his entire arm in thick cool mud to draw the poison out.

"What next, Cedric?" asked William.

The man was in severe pain, but it was localized at his arm thus far. "Now we wait, gentlemen," I said. "We will know in a moment if we are successful. I must loosen the strap and return blood to his arm, or he will lose his arm. But if I do this before the mud has drawn out the poison, it will spread, and he will die."

I looked for his wife, but she was gone. If we were successful, I wondered if I had condemned her to a slower, more painful death than her husband was facing. During such times, there is little time to think, only time to react. *What would the Prince do next*, I wondered.

Moments passed. The man was still breathing and had not gone mad. The mud was drying and the pain seemed to ease. I slowly loosened the leather strap and watched for the swelling to spread. The mud began to turn red from the new flow of blood to the cuts we had made in his arm. The swelling was contained, and we peeled the mud off. After washing his arm with clean water, we applied a clean bandage. Although his arm was twice its normal size, enough time had passed to know that he was not going to die. He wiped away the tears of pain that ran down his face.

We gave him some water to drink and leaned him against the front of his shop.

He whispered, "Who are you?"

"I am Cedric. This is William and Rob," I said. "We are Knights of the Prince."

He breathed deeply and closed his eyes. For the first time in many years, I could tell that his face was at peace from anger.

"Thank you! Thank you!" came a weak but sincere reply. "I do not know why anyone would bother to save the likes of me. Even my wife is gone, and I do not blame her."

"We have seen the compassion of the Prince and know that every man is worth saving," replied William.

"Will you listen to our story of his love for the kingdom and for you?" asked Rob.

"I am anxious to hear it, for I don't even know what kindness and love are. I have never seen nor felt them...until today," said the man.

"What is your name, sir?" I asked him.

"I am called Derek," he said. "Please, tell me of this man you call the Prince."

He was eager to hear our story of the King's great love for his people—a love so great that he sent his Son to teach us, and ultimately, to die for us. We told of the Prince's miraculous reappearance and of his promise to take us to a new kingdom where there is no hunger or despair. Each word of our story began to soften Derek's heart—a heart as hard as granite was slowly transformed to a heart ready to give and receive compassion. The story of the Prince does that to men. It breaks them down, removes the rubble, and builds a castle where there once was a prison.

Derek wiped more tears from his eyes. This time they were tears of repentance and joy.

"Please come to my house for a meal," Derek pleaded. "I want you to meet my family." Our story of the Prince gave Derek a chance to recover from the bite of the fire asp.

When he was ready, we traveled one street to the east of his shop and found ourselves approaching the door of his home. Two small, frightened faces peered out the window as we approached. When we entered his home, the children did not run to greet their father. They each darted to a corner to hide behind a piece of furniture. They were afraid of him. His wife, Cassy, was shocked that he was alive and slowly moved to the back of the room, fully expecting to be beaten for her abandonment.

Derek walked slowly toward his wife. She looked like a cornered mouse, too afraid to move. I thought she might collapse from her fear.

The little boy and girl knew what was to come, and they buried their heads in their knees and covered their ears with little hands.

"Cassy," said Derek in a hushed, quivering voice. Tears rushed to his eyes once again and flowed down his cheeks. "I am so very sorry." It was Derek that collapsed onto his knees before his wife. His large shoulders heaved with each sob. "How can you ever forgive me?" His hand reached to gently touch the hem of her tattered skirt.

Cassy's fear was replaced with bewilderment. She looked at Derek's bowed head for a moment, waiting for this horrible trick to end. She looked at her children and then to us in the doorway. I smiled and nodded to affirm the reality of Derek's transformed heart. She slowly moved her calloused hand to Derek's head. It was a gesture of forgiveness though she could not yet speak the words. Her eyes welled up with tears, and I knew her heart wanted to believe the unbelievable. How could years of abuse be stripped away in an afternoon? It was an emotional reconciliation for everyone.

The children were surprised at the silence and stole a peek to see their once violent father humbled on the floor before their mother. Derek looked up and beckoned for his children, but they too were hesitant to believe that their father would be anything but cruel. Slowly, they left their cover and cautiously approached Derek. The girl placed a protective arm around her little brother.

"Daddy," said the tender little voice of the small girl. "Please don't hurt us anymore." Her voice trembled knowing that such a plea usually only worsened her father's anger.

Derek carefully leaned forward to span the remaining distance between him and his children. He gently brought them into his arms, and his weeping deepened. "I promise I will never hurt you or your mother ever again," he said. "I love you, children." Their little arms wrapped around his neck as they felt their daddy's love for the first time.

Derek slowly stood and let Cassy look at his moist face. Her eyes were full and her lip quivered as she yielded her heart to the truth. Derek was a new man! The compassion of the King and the Prince had transformed him. His arms encircled her with the morning embrace of love.

"I love you, Cassy. I hope there's room left in your heart to love me...even just a little," said Derek.

"Oh, Derek!" said Cassy and she melted into his embrace. "I love you, too."

I leaned toward Rob. "This is why we must carry on, my brother!" I said. He smiled and nodded.

Chapter 14 - "Age of Darkness"

During the meal with Derek and his family, we shared the story of the Prince with Cassy and their children. They too understood, believed, and were born into a new life of hope. The spilled blood of the Prince grew love and compassion where there once was a desert. This family was transformed by his story, and I knew they would never be the same.

We left their home and traveled on to our destination in the North. Our mutual joy of sharing compassion with a family was uplifting but brief.

We passed a variety of shops and homes along the way. The usual bustle of activity on the streets paused for the turning of a page of sorrow. On every corner, a message was posted. It was a message to usher in a new age of darkness. At the street corners, small assemblies gathered, and the dust of the streets settled while all of Arrethtrae held its breath. We stopped to read:

Attention Citizens of Arrethtrae!

Governor Supreme Alexander Histen is hereby appointed King of Arrethtrae. ALL people will swear allegiance to King Alexander Histen and acknowledge his authority over all subjects by complying with the following proclamation.

1. All subjects will bow in the presence of King Alexander Histen.

2. All subjects will pay a permit fee to the King in exchange for the privilege of buying and selling goods in the kingdom of Arrethtrae. Upon the purchase of this permit, the King's insignia will be imprinted upon the subject's right hand. Any subject attempting to buy or sell goods without the imprint of the King will be punished!

3. No subject will acknowledge the existence of any authority other than King Alexander Histen. Violation of this order is punishable by death!

4. No subject is allowed to carry a sword without explicit approval of the King. All swords will be collected within the next two days.

5. No subject is allowed to travel beyond the limits of the city of which they reside without proper authorization from the King.

6. No subject is allowed to travel at night without proper authorization from the King.

Any subject who fails to comply with all points of this proclamation will be immediately punished.

All Hail King Alexander Histen!

We stood in silence as the severity of future persecution settled into our minds. Histen had attained total control. *What will happen to the Knights of the Prince?*, I wondered.

"Well, gentlemen, life just became very, very hard," commented William.

"Yes, it has," I said. "But what better time than now to spread the words of the Prince? The people will feel the iron hand of Histen and know bondage as they have never known it before. He is trying to strip the people of all hope, but we will give it to them. We will find a way to carry on. The Prince expects no less from us. Let us unite in an inseparable bond of brotherhood and fulfill our duty to the Code, the Prince, and the true King of Arrethtrae!"

I placed my hands on the shoulders of William and Rob. They too knew we must press on regardless of the dark situation in the kingdom. Too much was at stake for us to lose hope and give up.

"Let us not forget the promise of the Prince. He will return," I said to encourage them, as well as myself. William's jaw tightened in determination, and Rob nodded as we vowed to persevere no matter what the cost.

The grain of our vow was quickly tested. The new proclamation gave Histen's men renewed arrogance. Four of his men were collecting a "fee" from a shop owner across the street. This was a normal practice since Histen had come to power. However, this time the price was too much for the shop owner to bear.

"In addition to our fee, King Histen requires your daughter to come and serve in his palace," we heard the lead henchman state clearly to the man. He was the largest of the four and wore a black beard that was cut close to his skin. His thick chest and dark eyes made him look like quite a formidable foe. His three cohorts did not look as threatening, though sometimes looks are misleading. They sneered and obviously enjoyed the anguish they were about to cause this poor man and his daughter.

William, Rob, and I began to walk across the street toward the skirmish.

"I have paid you faithfully for over a year. I have even sworn allegiance to King Histen. My wife has died and my daughter is all that is important to me. You ask too much! I will not hand over my daughter to King Histen or to anyone else!" exclaimed the man.

"Then we will take her by force," said Histen's man. "Step aside!"

I heard a panicked scream from within the shop as the owner tried to stop the brutes from entering.

"Leave him alone!" I shouted at Histen's men.

Rob and William positioned themselves on my left and right, a few yards in front of the shop. The three of us were no longer amateur swordsmen. Over the past few years, we had honed our skills and fought many enemies. If I must fight a battle, I prefer William and Rob at my side. They are veterans and men of honor—men that I can trust.

The four men momentarily forgot their mission of plunder and turned to see what insolent fool dared to challenge them. The leader gazed harshly at us.

"Who dares challenge my authority and interfere in the King's business?" he threatened more than asked.

"No one you need be concerned with...as long as you leave the man and his daughter alone," said William.

"You are in violation of the King's proclamation. Hand over your swords immediately or you will be severely punished," came the leader's reply.

"We will give our swords to you, but you will not enjoy the manner in which they come," said Rob as his hand came to rest on the hilt of his sword.

The black bearded leader became enraged at our defiance and drew his sword from his scabbard. Within seconds, six swords slid from scabbards, filling the air with a brief harmony of sliding steel on steel. The leader spoke in hushed tones to one of the men, and the man withdrew slightly from the impending fight. Three of them charged, and we positioned ourselves. The bearded leader came for me.

I was challenged with my foe, as was William with his, but Rob gained the upper hand on his opponent quickly. He maneuvered him off to the left and away from the shop's door. The owner disappeared within, presumably to protect his daughter. From the corner of my eye, I saw the forth man exit to the east toward Histen's palace.

A strong blow came from my left. I blocked it with the flat of my sword and countered with a slice across the middle that grazed my enemy's right shoulder. He cursed but was not seriously injured, and he renewed his fight with vehemence. I saw Rob parry a weak cut and counter with a quick but lethal thrust that put his opponent down.

"Rob," I called between counters, "get the man and his daughter south to Barrett. I fear reinforcements are coming, so you'll have to move fast. We'll meet up with you there."

Rob entered the shop, and I turned my full attention to my opponent. William gained the upper hand, and his foe knew he was at his end. He backed off and ran east. The bearded leader knew the fight was out of his control and withdrew also. Down the street from the east, I saw a band of men coming speedily.

"You will pay for your treason with your lives!" screamed the leader.

We ran into the shop and locked the door. We exited through a back door into an alleyway. I saw Rob and his new companions at a distance to the south, but they were still vulnerable.

"William, we must stall Histen's men. We have to buy Rob enough time to get the man and his daughter to safety," I said.

The shouts of men were getting closer with each passing moment. We ran through another shop and onto a street parallel to the street on which the fight began. We ran north one street, then west—away from Histen's men. They followed as we had hoped, but we kept them at a safe distance. Finally, we lost our pursuers and found refuge in a small, unoccupied hut off the main streets.

William and I rested, waiting for Histen's men to abandon their search. It was some time before we ventured out again.

"I hope Rob was successful," said William.

"Yes, I do too," I replied. "Many hours have passed—ample time for them to reach safety. Let's take the back way out into the alley and start making our way home."

"I'm more than ready to go home, my friend," said William.

We slowly entered the alley, keeping a careful watch on the street just to the left of us. At last, there was no sign of a search, and we were relieved. The alley felt more secure than the street we were about to enter, or so I thought!

Behind us, a subdued, evil sounding chuckle broke my false hopes of seclusion. As we turned, the chuckle became a pompous, roaring laughter. Chills traveled up my spine. *It was Alexander Histen himself!* He was mounted on a black stallion, which snorted and flared its nostrils. On each side of Histen stood four of the largest warriors I have ever seen. All four men were darkly dressed with leather straps that crossed their chests. Each stood a full head taller than William or me. Obvious veterans of sword fighting, each owned a variety of scars. Their muscular frames alone were foreboding, but the massive and fiendish swords they carried finished the picture of undaunted destruction of which these men were clearly capable. We faced similar foes before—these were Shadow Warriors. Their brazen appearance with Histen told me one thing...the Dark Knight was near! Surely, this was the age of darkness of which the Prince spoke. I glanced at William and knew he felt the same fear I was fighting.

The four Shadow Warriors surrounded us to prevent any chance of escape. We instinctively stepped back toward the rock wall on the side of the alley. We thought that to draw our swords would mean quick and certain death.

Histen spoke in a thick, condescending tone. "Well, so this is Sir William and Sir Cedric of Chessington."

Although I had never seen Histen up close, he seemed as large as the Shadow Warriors. I was sure this perception was because he was mounted.

"Your little escapades around the kingdom are over!" he said as he dismounted the stallion.

As he approached, he seemed to grow with each stride until I realized my initial perception of his stature was true. Alexander Histen stood shoulder to shoulder with the Shadow Warriors. Unlike them, however, his face and exposed skin were free from any scars. His hair was jet-black and cut short. His facial features were sharp. He was well acquainted with authority, and it was clear he was the only author of all commands when present. His eyes were deep, dark, and penetrating.

"I am King of Arrethtrae. I will show mercy and allow you one chance to swear allegiance to me," said Histen.

In all my adventures as a Knight of the Prince, this was my most terrifying. My true fight was within myself—*fear*. With death staring me in the face, would my faith in the Prince give me the courage I needed to stand firm?

One of the Shadow Warriors drew his lethal sword, anxious to taste first blood. Two of them moved closer to us.

"Swear your allegiance and bow before me or die!" The words shot like poisoned darts. I slowly began to realize just how truly evil Histen was.

It was William that spoke first. "Our allegiance is to the Prince and his Father, the true King of Arrethtrae!" Though they were monstrous men, all four of them winced when William spoke of the Prince. Even his name was powerful!

The Shadow Warrior closest to William struck him on the brow of his head with the hilt of his sword. William fell to his knees and covered his head with his hands. Blood spilled between his fingers and onto the ground. Before I could kneel and help him, Histen stepped forward and gripped my neck with his left hand.

It was then I remembered the Prince's Silent Warriors. "The King reigns—and his Son!" I voiced what I could through Histen's tightening grip. Histen and the four Shadow Warriors bellowed in wicked laughter.

"The Silent Warriors will not save you, knave! I own this kingdom now. The former King and his weak Son are finished here." As Histen spoke, his heinous smile turned to a sneer full of loathing disgust. "I have finished them in Arrethtrae, and I will return one day to his own kingdom and kill them both!"

My fear, though I know not why, instantly left me. I knew I could stand and die with honor. Though Histen tried to demean the King and the Prince, his voice betrayed him, and I knew that Histen feared the Prince more than any fear I would ever feel from Histen.

"You are not the true king of Arrethtrae," I boldly said. "You have betrayed the people and lied to them. You only care for power and control. You are not who the people think you are...I see what a truly evil leader you are."

Histen glared at me with eyes that spewed hatred like poison from a viper. His hand tightened around my neck, nearly closing off my air. I felt the rocks in the wall behind me press into my head and back. He leaned into my face. His handsome features were twisted into a gut wrenching evil countenance. My vision started to blur, and my mind was beginning to fade. In my waning, I saw a vision of the Prince standing on the roof of the building across the alleyway. *Unconsciousness must not be far away*, I thought.

"You are right about one thing, peasant," Histen spoke in a deep guttural voice that was nearly a whisper. "I am not who the people think I am." He wanted to kill me. I never knew hate could so completely possess a man. "I..." his grip tightened, "...am"— tighter; I could not breathe now, "...Lucius!" His right hand revealed a deadly dagger that would soon spill my blood. He pulled back to strike. From the corner of my eye, I saw one of the Shadow Warriors raise his sword to slay William, still face down on the ground.

This was the end, I thought. I was to die at the hands of Lucius—the evil enemy of the Prince. In my final moments, the vision of the Prince seemed so real. His sword was drawn, and he beckoned me to...to...fight?!

The dagger started its deadly plunge toward my chest. Time nearly froze. I could not let the Prince down and die such a feeble death. He trained me for this very fight—a fight against the evil one.

The dagger flashed closer.

Maybe I would die, but only after exhausting every fiber of strength and will in my body. *Yes, my Prince, I will fight...fight for you,* I thought.

The deadly dagger was nearing its target—my heart. With all my strength and speed, I rotated my left forearm from my right and across my chest to deflect the dagger, now only inches from my chest, and simultaneously rotated my body. It was just enough— the dagger skinned my left shoulder and impacted the rocks behind me.

My body was turned slightly to the left and my right hand found the hilt of my sword in an instant. I heard Lucius curse and recoil for another strike, but I beat him to it. My left hand joined my right at my sword as I partially withdrew it from my scabbard with great force. My fisted hands and the hilt of my sword struck Lucius' stomach. His suffocating grip on my neck was immediately broken as he doubled over from the blow.

"MOVE, WILLIAM!" I shouted as I saw the blade of the Shadow Warrior descend on him. William rolled with the speed of a panther. The sword missed William and hit the ground with tremendous force—a shower of sparks flew in all directions.

There was a moment of chaos that allowed me to spring toward William's position. My sword was now fully drawn, and I lunged at the Shadow Warrior that was making another strike at William as he tried to scramble to his feet. My sword found its deadly mark, and the Shadow Warrior collapsed in an instant.

Lucius tried to give orders, but the air had left his lungs; he could only make gestures toward us.

William was now on his feet with his sword drawn. We were side-by-side and ready to fight, though we knew it would be our last. The three remaining Shadow Warriors advanced quickly—then hesitated. I knew they were looking past us to something that was approaching from behind. I did not dare to turn and look, lest the monstrous brutes before us take advantage of the distraction.

"Good afternoon, gentlemen," came Rob's familiar voice from my right. "It looks like you are in need of some assistance."

Rob joined to my right and Barrett to William's left.

"We will fight for the Prince and for our brothers," stated Barrett.

Our brief moment of relief quickly transformed into the seriousness of battle with our brothers in arms. Rob and Barrett joined us to either save us or to die with us. There was no worse enemy than this, and we all knew it.

"*KILL THEM!*" shouted Lucius. His lungs had recovered and his wrath was obvious. We took our stance and prepared for the onslaught, but they still held back.

"They were trained by the Prince," said one of the Shadow Warriors over his shoulder. He did not take his eyes off of us.

Lucius moved forward with his sword drawn. "Attack or I will kill you myself!" he yelled to his men as he lunged toward me. The Shadow Warriors followed... each one to one of us—the battle began.

The rage on Lucius' face matched the fury of his sword. It was a duel to the death, and I knew I must rely on the training of the Prince. Lucius was quick and cunning. Our swords met in a ferocious volley of thrusts, cuts, and slices. The Prince had prepared me for this battle, and I was ready. I saw the Prince in every motion of my sword. My muscles had memorized the moves, and my sword seemed to know exactly what to do. I felt the Prince in my arms and hands—I gave control to him. My sword flew to match each cut and thrust of this beast. The sword of the Prince would protect me...deliver me. My confidence through the battle was surreal; all fear was gone. I was trained by the master himself..."The Master of the Sword!"

The close quarters of the alleyway forced the four separate sword fights to spread out. The clashing swords echoed off the walls, which added to the intensity of the battle. I saw Rob take a cut across his shoulder, but it was not deep. He, William, and Barrett fought like the valiant warriors they were trained to be. The Shadow Warriors were huge, but we were fast and knew their tricks. The battle raged on.

Lucius thrust—I parried and countered, but he caught my cut with the flat of his sword. He quickly countered with a cut across my chest. *Whoosh!* I leaped back to miss his blade and lost my balance. I fell to my knees. Lucius pounced toward me with a vertical cut that I caught with my sword just above my head. I threw my left leg in a circular motion to trip him—his legs flew out from under him. I seized the opportunity to scramble to my feet. Lucius recovered quickly, and we engaged our swords again.

I saw William counter a cut with a quick thrust—it found its mark. The Shadow Warrior dropped his sword and clutched his chest as he fell to the ground.

William was closest to Barrett and joined him against his foe. The fight quickly turned in our favor, and I saw the contempt on Lucius' face grow more vivid with each passing moment. He backed off quickly as Barrett's opponent fell from a fatal wound. The last Shadow Warrior turned and ran up the alley. Lucius quickly mounted his stallion and galloped away.

"I will be back to kill all of you!" he screamed with vehemence.

"Praise to the King and his Son, the Prince!" we shouted in return. The battle was over...the Knights of the Prince prevailed. We breathed a temporary sigh of relief, but then we realized we were still a long way from home.

"Thank you, gentlemen," I said to Rob and Barrett. "You came not a moment too soon."

"I was worried when you didn't show at Barrett's, so we decided to come for you," said Rob as Barrett bandaged his arm.

"And I'm glad you did," said William gratefully. He looked a mess because of the blood from his initial head wound. The bleeding had nearly stopped, and I washed the cut with clean water.

"I don't know about you, gentlemen, but I'm ready to go home," I said. The rush of the fight was leaving my body. I was tired...bone tired.

On our journey back south, we moved carefully, avoiding all possible contact with people. I thought about the dark shadow that now hung over Arrethtrae. Lucius' power was going to grow with each passing day. These were becoming dark days indeed. *My Prince, when will you return?* I thought...I yearned.

Chapter 15 - "Taken!"

"Awake, Cedric!" the words sounded hollow and distant. I tried to understand them, but my mind refused. I found that place in sleep so deep and peaceful that one would rather have a roof fall on him than awaken. I sensed a tugging on my arm and fought to gain consciousness, but my recovery was slow.

"It is time. We must go immediately. Wake up!" My eyes focused on the massive frame bent over me.

"Keef, is that you?" I asked groggily.

"Yes, my old friend," said Keef. "The time has come to go home. Rise up and come with me. We are all going home!" I thought I saw him return an object to his pouch.

My limbs felt as heavy as lead, but I managed to grab his arm, and he swung me to my feet.

"It is very good to see you, Keef," I smiled and wiped away the sleep. "What is happening?"

"It is the King," said Keef. "He has called us all home to his kingdom. The Silent Warriors are spread throughout the land and are gathering the Knights of the Prince this very moment. Ships are waiting for us. We must move everyone quickly and quietly before the Dark Knight discovers us."

I wondered how Keef and the other Silent Warriors were able to orchestrate such a rescue and exodus so quietly and smoothly.

"Hurry, Cedric," said Keef. "We must move quickly. Do not take anything except your sword. Move toward the ships at the docks. You must not speak to anyone until you reach the ships."

"Why not, Keef?" I asked. "Shouldn't I help you gather the knights?"

"That is not possible, Cedric," responded Keef. "You see, not everyone who claims to be for the Prince will be taken. The Silent Warriors have been watching everyone claiming to be a Knight of the Prince, and we know who is truly one of his followers."

Keef read my concern as I thought of all the people I had labored to reach in the kingdom for the Prince. Who would be missing when I got to the ships?

"I'm sorry, Cedric," said Keef. "I must leave now and gather more of the knights. I will see you across the sea, my friend. Take care and do not waste any time. The Prince awaits you!"

"Farewell, Keef," I nodded as we exited my home. He turned north.

I turned south toward the docks. *Please*, I thought, *let all of my close brothers be there.* I walked a few paces and turned back to ask Keef a final question, but he was already gone. Did he say the Prince awaits or was my mind still foggy with sleep?

There was a silent exodus of people out of the city. Men, women, and children sprinkled the streets and alleyways—all heading south to the docks. As I moved, I couldn't help but increase my speed with each step. Would the Prince be waiting at the ships, or must I wait until after the voyage to see my friend, my teacher, my Lord?

I recognized most of the people silently making their way to the ships and smiled a salutation. I stopped to help carry a little boy belonging to a family with six children. Mom's and Dad's arms were already full of smaller sleeping children. It slowed my pace, but I did not care. We were all going home!

I wondered how we could possibly get everyone out of the city without being discovered. Surely someone would awaken and reveal our flight. As these thoughts occupied my mind, I nearly tripped over a motionless body on the side of the street. I stopped to help, thinking this person was one of our own and was hurt. As I bent closer to the body, I realized it was a man sleeping so heavily that he nearly seemed dead. I later learned that the Silent Warriors had tainted all drinking water with a sleeping compound. The entire kingdom was asleep and would stay that way for many hours. Even we were affected, but the Silent Warriors possessed a counter agent to awaken us.

The little boy I was carrying was now fully awake and asked to walk on his own. I set him by his father's side. He smiled in gratitude, and I moved on at my previous quickened pace. As I approached the docks, I saw two ships already underway out to sea. They were full of fellow knights. The silent mass of people flowed steadily from the streets and onto the ships, all of them passing by one man—*the Prince!*

I could not contain my enthusiasm. My quickened pace turned to a full run. No longer was he wearing the clothes of a peasant. He was now clothed in full royal attire which framed his majestic character. His magnificent sword hung near his side. The sight of him demanded awe and respect. This was only a glimpse of what he gave up to set us free. Soon I would see the splendor of his kingdom and all its riches. He did this for me! My mind could hardly grasp that statement as truth. The King and his Son must love us more than we thought possible—more than we could love even our own children. What a strange way to save the kingdom!

The Prince looked at me as I came to him. Those same penetrating eyes smiled at me. Tears spilled onto my cheeks as I knelt before him and took in his loving gaze. Just as he once before lowered himself for me as a peasant, he knelt to one knee and put his hand behind my neck.

His voice was quiet and sincere. "Well done, Cedric. Well done!"

I lowered my head and wept. Oh, how I craved to hear those words. They were the prize for all my journeys…all my struggles. I cherish them to this day more than gold. The Prince raised me to my feet and hugged me as though I were his son. I was already home!

Chapter 16 - "The Great Battle"

Our arrival in the kingdom across the sea was glorious. William and I shared our stories with many fellow knights, and the Silent Warriors captivated us with all they had seen and experienced as well. One particularly joyful reunion was with my old friend Leinad. He had devoted his entire life to loyal service of the King. I listened to all of his grand adventures as a gallant knight once again, but this time I was spellbound because those stories were so significant to the arrival of the Prince.

After the great reunion and celebration, we continued our training under the Prince once again. He was preparing us—preparing us for this very day...this very battle.

Now you know my story. I was but a peasant, hungry and clothed in rags. Today I share the line of gallant knights—Knights of the Prince. I wear the armor of the Prince and will fight beside him this hour. This is where you found me, and this is where I must leave you...at the kingdom's edge. This is the battle to regain Arrethtrae. Never in the history of man was there ever a battle between such powerful forces, nor will there ever be again. The Dark Knight must be conquered!

After our departure from Arrethtrae, the Dark Knight used our mysterious disappearance to further frighten the people and secure his total control over the entire kingdom. He was in his own perverted glory for a time. Fear ruled the people. If they did not serve him, they

were eliminated. But now his time is come…the Prince
will make sure of that.

There is the Prince now—his white stallion beneath
and his magnificent sword before! Nothing
can stand before the Prince. He is truly
invincible.

The sound of a mighty and evil force
approaches, but I am not afraid. I am on the
side of the Prince. On whose side are you?

The End

"Deliverance"

Music by Emily Elizabeth Black
Lyrics by Chuck Black
Edited by Brittney Dyanne Black

Deliverance

Written for Kingdom's Edge

Music by Emily Elizabeth Black
Lyrics by Chuck Black
Edited by Brittney Dyanne Black

Oo- Ah-

Come see the man from a dis-tant land. Come hear his words of hope. He speaks of a king-dom of the heart, call-ing all to be a part.

Oo- Ah- Come see the man from a dis-tant land. Cham-pion of poor and meek. His words of truth no-ble men des-pise. See how now he

gives his life.

ff Will hope die? Free-dom cries! *mp*

Oo- Ah- Come see the man of de-liv-er-ance.

Death has no hold on him! No-ble, right-teous, ro-yal Son of King! Prince and Lord of

every-thing!

Much Slower

Oo- Ah- He lives! He lives! He lives a-gain!

Commentary

The power of a parable is dramatic. The words you've just read are original, but the story is not. Nearly every scene in the book represents a specific event that took place 2000 years ago. This story can be read for simple enjoyment or for the deeper spiritual analogies to the single most significant event in human history. Please read on if you are curious about understanding these analogies.

The basis of the story is obviously focused on Jesus Christ, the Prince, and his three year ministry, his sacrifice, and his resurrection. As mere men, the disciples then, and us now, have found it difficult to grasp the reality of warfare in the spirit world. Although that warfare is as real as the sword fights that occurred during the Middle Ages, this story attempts to bring that spiritual warfare into a more comprehensible physical world.

The Bible teaches that our only offensive weapon against Satan and his demons is the Word of God (Ephesians 6:17). The climactic duel of the universe occurred when Satan tempted Jesus in the wilderness. The fate of all mankind was on his shoulders. Jesus was victorious because he used Scripture, his sword, in each temptation (Matthew 4:1-11). It is a perfect example for us to follow, but we must have a sword, and the sword must be sharpened and polished as Cedric did in preparation for his battles. The sword is therefore a point of primary focus throughout the story.

Hebrews 4:12 states:

"For the word of God is quick, and powerful, and sharper than any two-edged sword, piercing even to the dividing asunder of soul and spirit, and of the joints and marrow, and is a discerner of the thoughts and intents of the heart."

The sword represents the Word of God but *only* the Word of God. The Pharisees had God's Word also but Jesus was fiercely disappointed with them. What they lacked was the true meaning or the intent of God's Word. Thus, the Code represents the true meaning of God's Word. The Noble Knights, representing the Pharisees, used their swords to esteem themselves and therefore failed the King and the people. The sword is used to defeat evil but also to show compassion and love to the humble and weak. God's Word should be written on our hearts and should not be just a set of rules to be followed.

Cedric represents all men, women, and children who have trusted in Jesus Christ as Lord and Savior. He spans the age from Peter to the last person "called" before we are taken home. Hopefully, the reader will see himself or herself as Cedric, whom the Prince chose to elevate from spiritual poverty to heir of his heavenly kingdom. Cedric is an unlikely knight because he is poor and untrained just as we are unlikely candidates to be children of God because of our sinful natures. It is only through the love, power, and sacrifice of Jesus that we are made worthy.

Other personifications include Kifus, who represents Caiaphas, the high priest (Matthew 26:57). The Silent Warriors are God's holy angels and the Shadow

Warriors are Satan's demons. The Dark Knight, Lucius, represents Lucifer and the beast of the end times. Leinad represents the prophets that brought God's Word to the people.

Some scene analogies include the temptation of Christ, the miraculous feeding of the hungry, Jesus' love for children, the casting out of demons, the crucifixion, the resurrection, and the rapture. There are more analogies throughout the story. In fact, nearly every word, scene, and name was written with symbolism and analogy in mind. Revealing all would leave no mystery or challenge for your second reading.

The final battle that is about to take place as the story begins and ends is the ultimate battle between good and evil. Jesus will defeat Satan and his demons once and for all. If you have trusted Jesus as your Lord and Savior, you are a Child of God—a saint. As the saints of God, we will be a part of that victorious army. For the interim, let us put on the whole armor of God and wage war of eternal significance as a soldier for our Lord and Savior Jesus Christ.

"Finally, my brethren, be strong in the Lord, and in the power of his might. Put on the whole armour of God, that ye may be able to stand against the wiles of the devil."

Ephesians 6:10-11

If this book has been a blessing to you, please consider ordering additional copies for your friends and family. A convenient order form is on the following page.

Please fill out and mail a copy of the order form below.

ORDER FORM

QNTY	DESCRIPTION	EACH	TOTAL
	Kingdom's Dawn	$9.95	
	Kingdom's Hope	$9.95	
	Kingdom's Edge	$9.95	
	Kingdom's Reign	$9.95	
	Kingdom Series 4 Book Set (10% Discount)	$35.80	
	Kingdom's Dawn Audio Book Drama (3 disc set)	$19.95	
	Kingdom's Hope Audio Book Drama (3 disc set)	$19.95	
	Sales Tax (ND residents add 5%)		
	Shipping & Handling		
	Total		

~Send Check & Order Form to:
Perfect Praise Publishing
1228 4th Ave East
Williston, ND 58801

~Or call (701) 572-1700 to order
by credit card.

~Or order online at
www.kingdomseries.com

USPS Shipping & Handling Charges	
1 book	$2.50
2 books	$3.00
3-5 books	$3.50
6-10 books	$5.00
>10 books	*FREE!*

Send books to:
Your Name:
Your Address:
City, State & Zip:
Phone:
Email:

www.kingdomseries.com